CHANGING THE ATTITUDE
OF CHRISTIAN TOWARD JEW

CHANGING THE ATTITUDE
of CHRISTIAN
toward JEW

A PSYCHOLOGICAL APPROACH
THROUGH RELIGION

By *HENRY ENOCH KAGAN*

1952
Columbia University Press, New York

PUBLISHED IN GREAT BRITAIN, CANADA, AND INDIA
BY GEOFFREY CUMBERLEGE, OXFORD UNIVERSITY PRESS
LONDON, TORONTO, AND BOMBAY

MANUFACTURED IN THE UNITED STATES OF AMERICA

To My Beloved Family

ESTHER

JONATHAN

AND

JEREMY

FOREWORD

FOR centuries Jews have been trying to teach Christians about Jews. And Christians have been trying to teach Jews about Christians. To what avail? Judged in terms of mutual understanding and trust the success seems slender indeed.

The author of this timely book says in effect: Let us analyze the problem of interfaith education scientifically. Let us no longer assume that our expenditure of good will and effort automatically leads to an improvement in group relations. As a beginning, we may take two basic styles of teaching and evaluate their results. Does either of them make for more friendly attitudes?

The first style Dr. Kagan calls *indirect*. It represents full-bodied teaching in the traditional sense, devoid of direct efforts at therapy. Under it the students learn about the literature of the Psalms or other portions of the Old Testament and are led to understand their spiritual purport for both Jewish and Christian culture. The students are Christian; their teacher is a scholarly Rabbi who lends to the lessons they learn the prestige of a friendly out-group authority. The method is indirect because it does not include discussions of anti-Semitism nor invite the student to explore his own attitudes toward the Jew. Does such an educational arrangement affect these attitudes at all?

The second style is *direct*. It includes many of the features of the indirect method, but adds frank group discussion of contemporary anti-Jewish attitudes. In the course of such discussion the student may find himself talking about his own hostility and may conceivably gain cathartic benefits and grow in insight.

A variant of the direct method is the *focused interview* wherein the student instead of discussing his own views in the group does so in a private conference with the Rabbi. Here the method used in class is indirect, but each individual student has the added opportunity of talking privately about his own experiences with Jews and about Christian-Jewish relations.

In carrying out this interesting experimental design Dr. Kagan worked with groups of adolescents in summer church camps (Episcopalian and Methodist). The courses of instruction were brief, lasting only for five days. Thus the time was short and the subjects highly selected and presumably impressionable (although by no means free from anti-Semitism).

Under these limited conditions the author obtains strong evidence in favor of the direct method. Indeed the indirect approach proves to be essentially worthless so far as the building of friendly attitudes toward the Jew is concerned. The focused interview seems to approach the direct method in positive results—a somewhat surprising finding in view of the short half-hour period of private conference allotted to each student. The author adds, however, that the direct method surpasses the focused interview method in giving stability over time to the favorable change. The direct method likewise seems to add a sense of group support to the favorable change in attitudes, with the result that the lessons learned carry over to an appreciable degree into everyday conduct—and do not remain limited to verbal performance on questionnaire items.

The author wisely employs many scientific safeguards in his research. He uses control groups (students who are given no class instruction whatever). With due regard for individual differences he pays attention to the fact that certain students respond in quite opposite ways to the same type of instruction. He uses standard tests of statistical significance, and examines carefully the question whether his questionnaire instrument corresponds to the students' behavior in everyday life. Furthermore, he studies the stability of attitude change over an eight months interval of time. This self-critical examination of method inspires confidence in the final results.

Of course, we do not yet know whether the direct method of approach—facing anti-Semitism frankly in a discussion group—will reduce prejudice for all types of peoples under all types of conditions. From our previous knowledge of the diversity of human groups and from the author's own data, we may doubt that this formula will always have precisely the same effects. Nevertheless, the results already create grave difficulty for those who hold that the most effective way to handle prejudice is to overlook its existence or to engage merely in factual education that will blanket —and presumably smother—hostile attitudes.

To my mind this modest experiment is worth more than a thousand pages of exhortation and speculation concerning intergroup relations. In the modern spirit of critical evaluation it dispenses with both pious wish and educational dogmatism. Employing the best available resources of social science it measures change in attitude resulting from concretely defined programs of education. Not only are the results suggestive for guiding future educational practice, but the method developed and the objective spirit of the enterprise give us a model for research. If we follow this model, we should soon know, far better than we do now, how to educate for better relationships within the human family.

GORDON W. ALLPORT

Harvard University
June, 1951

PREFACE

"Finally, brethren, whatsoever things are true, whatsoever things are honest, whatsoever things are just, whatsoever things are pure, whatsoever things are lovely, whatsoever things are of good report; if there be any virtue, and if there be any praise, think on these things."—PHILIPPIANS, IV:8.

ESCRIPTIONS of the history, the symptoms, and the causes of anti-Semitism may be found in innumerable volumes. Prescriptions for the cure of anti-Semitism are few. A deeply rooted prejudice, hatred of the Jew, is further complicated by conscious and subconscious religious emotions. Heretofore, the anti-Jewish attitude could not be approached by experimentation similar to that which science requires for arriving at a tested therapy for any illness. Christians admitting anti-Jewish prejudice would have to submit themselves to experiments designed to eliminate or at least reduce their prejudice. To the author's knowledge, this is the first time that professing Christians have made themselves available to the social scientist for experimenting in methods for *changing* their attitudes toward the Jew.

To the five hundred and twenty-five Christian men and women who are the subjects of this book and to the Methodist Church of America and the Episcopal Diocese of Connecticut, under whose auspices these young people became my students, I wish to express my most profound gratitude. Shocked out of complacency by the demoniac bestiality of Nazi anti-Semitism and its universal threat to Christianity and democracy, these Protestant denominations together with thoughtful leaders throughout the Christian Church are seriously undertaking the most difficult task of trying to root out the age-old Christian animus against the Jew. In the vanguard in this spiritual battle is the National Conference of Christians and Jews. I wish to acknowledge the encouragement of two of its dedicated leaders, Dr. Everett R. Clinchy and Reverend Willard L. Johnson, who manifested great interest throughout the progress of my investigations. It is my earnest hope that all the Christians who have participated in this study as well as Christian readers of this book will find the objectivity of its psychological-religious approach characterized by a high regard for their Christian faith.

Like other sciences, psychology requires an instrument for measuring change. Complicated statistical techniques have been developed for establishing the validity of a scale to measure degrees of prejudice. While these procedures hold special interest for the psychologist, the general reader may find it advisable to omit the statistical parts of this book. This will not affect the continuity of the text. In Chapter II, the general reader may wish to read only the sixteen questions which comprise the Scale for Measuring Attitude Toward the Jew. Throughout the other chapters he may omit the statistical tables and read only the conclusions.

To a number of specialists this book may have particular interest. The religious teacher, the Christian clergyman, and the Rabbi, may find the psychological consequences of the ambivalent relationship between Judaism and Christianity, the semantics of the term "Old Testament," and the new techniques used in teaching Bible to effect changes in attitude valuable for his spiritual ministrations to spread good will. The psychologist may examine the validity of the attitude scale, the dynamics of the group cathartic method, and the religious factor so widely ignored in the modern analysis of anti-Semitism. The expert in public relations may be interested in the proof of how ineffectual is informational propaganda for improving Christian-Jewish relations. More effective programs as suggested by the findings of this study might be undertaken by Jewish organizations engaged in "defense work."

While the author takes full responsibility for the results and the shortcomings of this experiment, little could have been accomplished without the guidance of a number of outstanding scholars. I owe my greatest debt to Professor Goodwin Watson for his sympathetic supervision of this study. To Professors Martin Chworowsky, S. Stansfeld Sargent, Irving D. Lorge, and the late Ruth Benedict for their advice regarding psychological and statistical procedures and to Professor Salo Baron for his counsel on Jewish content, I wish to express my sincere appreciation and thanks. For editorial assistance in the preparation of the manuscript I am grateful to Elizabeth E. Adams, Esther Ruth Miller, and Dorothy Shapiro.

The publication of this book was made possible through the generous support of Mr. Roger Williams Straus, who has labored with constant diligence and consecrated devotion to the cause of better understanding among the racial and religious groups that compose our American citizenry. In the preface to his thoughtful book of essays on *Religious Liberty and Democracy* Mr. Straus, with realistic insight, pointed out how necessary it is "that proper techniques be developed to advance the cause of brotherly love." It is my earnest hope that the techniques established by this book will mark a step forward in that advance.

HENRY E. KAGAN

Mount Vernon, New York
September 4, 1951

CONTENTS

CONTENTS

I. INTRODUCTION

THE RELIGIOUS FRAME OF REFERENCE

HOW can hostile attitudes toward the Jew be changed? One must first find out whether those who have prejudices against Jews desire to be relieved of these feelings. They might be moved to change their anti-Jewish attitudes if they could be made aware that, by these prejudices, they repudiate their own principles. To develop an effective method for reducing prejudice, one must consider, therefore, the beliefs with which the prejudice is in conflict. Within what set of values does a Christian's prejudice against a Jew operate?

Anti-Semitism functions in Western Christian society. It is incompatible with the political affirmations as well as with the religious professions of that culture. Deeply involved in the development of American political democracy is the religious belief that the individual is entitled to equality. Rights belong to each individual by *sacred* sanction. "We hold these truths to be self-evident that all men are created equal; that they are endowed by their Creator with certain inalienable rights, that among these are life, liberty and the pursuit of happiness." This political-religious declaration sets forth a social superego which makes the highest ethical demands on Americans; and Gunnar Myrdal has drawn attention to the guilt feelings which trouble Americans when discriminatory practices against racial and religious minorities conflict with this American Creed.

Considerable effort is now being expended on high governmental levels to resolve the guilt of discrimination. This activity to improve the treatment of all minorities in America has been intensified as a result of World War II. America's need for internal solidarity as well as its ideological war against the Nazi and Japanese doctrines of racial superiority served to stimulate a program to make domestic practices conform more closely to American idealism. The present postwar impetus to correct injustices against minority groups comes partly from the pressure of the minorities themselves and partly from the challenge to American prestige in international relations since America's moral leadership in world affairs is colored by its treatment of its own minority groups.

More democratic patterns of behavior are now being proposed for the American community. These are to be implemented by certain laws and court actions for the protection of minorities against disenfranchisement, segregation, and discrimination in employment and education. Such political manipulations might become more effective if they were accompanied by more favorable attitudes on the part of the majority toward the minority. Since changes in attitudes will reinforce action programs, the educational work being done by many national and local organizations to improve intergroup understanding is of considerable importance. Recently, Goodwin Watson, Charles S. Johnson, and Robin M. Williams, Jr. evaluated and classified the different methods employed by these organizations for modifying intergroup antagonisms (Watson, 1946; Johnson, 1946; Williams, 1947).

As for the hostile attitudes of Christians toward Jews, the techniques for their reduction must take into consideration religious ideas. Both the why and the how of changing anti-Jewish feelings are determined by what a Jew is and by the values which a Christian, active or nominal, possesses. The values of a Christian are religious and the definition of the Jew includes a religious identification. The frame of reference is set by the relationship between two religions, Judaism and Christianity.

Whatever the sources of friction between Jew and Christian— the economic, the socio-political, the psychological—they cannot be separated from an historical and contemporary religious context. It is true that individual Jews are in economic competition with individual Christians. The world financial controls attributed to Jews as a group is, of course, mythological. Nonetheless, individual Jews successful in prestige occupations supply a rationalization for such economic theories about Jews. These false theories based on the economic prejudice of writers like Werner Sombart enjoy popular appeal during periods of economic depression. As Miriam Beard states, "some of the most dangerous delusions have been propagated by a renowned economic historian, Werner Sombart, whose book *Die Juden und das Wirtschaftsleben* gave as much support to Hitlerism as the works of Gobineau or Lothrop Stoddard" (the racialists) (Graeber and Britt, 1942, p. 363).

It is true that though the Jew is in many situations less of an immigrant than the Christian, he may still be considered an "outsider." His bi-cultural characteristics, which make him a native and a Jew, keep the Jew in a marginal social position so that the antagonism between the non-Jewish in-group and the Jewish out-group persists no matter how well the Jew is "assimilated." This social antagonism becomes aggravated by political crisis, for part of the mechanism for stirring up national patriotism to meet economic or military threat is to focus attention on the vulnerable "stranger" as a symbol of the danger.

It is further true that personal frustrations caused by economic disability, by social insecurity, and by cultural inhibition will generate free-floating aggressions within a person. Since revenge against the real causes of the frustrations may have to be repressed either because the real causes are not sufficiently known or because such action would bring on retaliation, these aggressions seek substitute outlets. They will be directed against targets which involve no risk of reprisal. A socially acceptable target for the displacement of repressed aggression has long been the ubiquitous, highly visible, and formerly defenseless Jew. When aggression is deflected away from the real frustrating object on to an innocent scapegoat, guilt feelings arise in the aggressor. Effort is then made to evade these guilt feelings by projecting them on to the Jew. The aggressor, to conceal his own shame, declares the Jew guilty; he finds "reasons" for blaming the Jew to account for his own unreasonable behavior toward the Jew (Dollard, 1939).

One cannot oversimplify the complex phenomenon of anti-Semitism by attributing it to any single factor. All these factors, the economic, the socio-political and the psychological reinforce each other to create a field of forces in which hostility against Jews grows.

Yet, these interlocking factors alone are insufficient to account for the *particular* selection of the Jews as the target for aggression. Any factor, including the economic, if it is to have any effect upon group prejudice must presuppose the existence of the psychological prior division into an in-group and an out-group (MacCrone, 1937, p. 254). The Jews have always been differentiated. They stand out because they are the only non-Christians of appreciable number in a Christian culture. Against them there has been a long-established religious habit-system of antipathy.

One is impressed by the fact that no matter by what separate branch of the social sciences an analysis of anti-Semitism is attempted, its religious aspect is invariably included. The economists, the sociologists, the political scientists, the anthropologists, and the psychologists writing in the symposium *Jews in a Gentile World* edited by Graeber and Britt, all find themselves confronted with the subject of the religious character of the Jew (Graeber and Britt, 1942). It is this religious characteristic which first defines the Jew as an out-group member in the dominantly Christian society, and there is something unique in this religious differentiation. The Jew has a religion which is strikingly different from Christianity and at the same time he has a religion which is the indispensable foundation of Christianity.

Because Judaism both resembles Christianity and differs from it, the Christian's attitude toward the religion of the Jews is ambivalent. He accepts the common religious ideology and rejects the Jew for insisting on his distinctive religious identity. "Most persons," observes J. O. Hertzler, "find it difficult to forgive those who differ from their religious faith. The reason probably is that since all religion is in the realm of the unknowable and unprovable, any divergent religious belief is in the nature of a criticism, even a denial of that held by the majority" (Graeber and Britt, 1942, p. 68). This hostile predisposition on the part of a Christian toward a Jew, which the continued existence of Judaism arouses, can even become aggravated by the fact that Christian and Jew share in common the belief in the same God and the same holy book, the Old Testament. The friction is in the nature of a family quarrel and therefore creates more hostility than it would if the strangeness between Christian and Jew were based on the lack of all common tradition (Graeber and Britt, 1942, p. 115).

The average Christian may not be aware of the ambivalent nature of his feelings toward Jews. However, there certainly is a dialectic basis in the religious literature for a Christian's liking and disliking Jews. This ambivalence is derived from the theological relations between Christianity and Judaism. To prepare for the coming of God's Kingdom of justice and peace to supplant the world of hate and war, the Jew is supposed to be "chosen." As the chosen, the Jews must be a "holy nation" unlike other nations. From this doctrine has come the non-Jew's contempt for the arrogance of the Jew's claim to superiority in the matter of salvation. This contempt was true of the pre-Christian pagan as well as of the Christian. As the result of this very contempt, the suffering of the Jew became a part of Jewish theology itself. It is an inseparable corollary of the privilege of being the "chosen people." As God's servant the Jew "is despised and rejected of men; a man of sorrows and acquainted with grief" (Isaiah 53:2, 3). In this second doctrine there is an enigmatic justification for the persecution of the Jews. However, because of still a third thesis, the doctrine of eschatology, the Jew must be preserved until his mission is fulfilled by the sudden and miraculous arrival of God's Messianic Kingdom. Thus, traditional Jewish theology is itself ambivalent for it holds that though the Jew must suffer, he nonetheless is loved by God.

The ambivalent attitude of Christianity toward Judaism is derived from this ambivalent nature of Jewish theology. According to Christianity, the failure of the Jews to recognize Jesus as the Messiah or Christ had both a negative and a positive result. On the one hand, the Jews are now supposed to be rejected by God. On the other hand, the very condemnation of the Jews was the "good fortune" of the Gentiles since it gave them the opportunity to become converted to Christianity instead of Judaism (Romans 11:11). Furthermore, Christian theology could not conceive that God should irretrievably condemn the people He once chose. "Has God cast away His people?" is asked in Romans; "God forbid. . . . As concerning the Gospel they are enemies . . . but as touching the election they are beloved for the fathers' sake" (Romans 11:1, 28). Thus, it is still true that despite the Jews' refusal to accept Jesus as Christ, "Salvation is of the Jews" (John 4:22), for when all the Gentiles are converted to Christianity the Jews will then see the light and the division between Church and Synagogue will eventually disappear. "For if the casting away of them (the Jews) be the reconciling of the world what shall the receiving of them be but life from the dead" (Romans 11:15). This accounts for the Medieval Church's depicting the Synagogue in a symbolic statue as blindfolded but still standing beside the figure representing the Church. Because of a divine plan of ultimate salvation, the Jew is despised and may be persecuted but he must be preserved. In this manner, as Carl Mayer develops this thesis, the "Jewish problem" became a cardinal paradox in Christian theology (Graeber and Britt, 1942, p. 322).

The Christian doctrine that the Jewish group must never disappear originates in that pristine period of Christianity when Christian and Jew were one and the same. Neither Jesus nor his disciples desired the extinction of their own people. On the contrary, Jesus believed he was strengthening Judaism when, for example, he criticized hypocrisy. Even Paul, though he said harsh things against Jewish Law, spoke proudly of his Jewish descent and his Pharisaic training. In fact, Paul broadened the term "Jew" to include the fellowship of those converted pagans who lived by the new Christian faith. In those days, Christianity was a Jewish sect within the religious society of Judaism (Parkes, 1948, Chaps. II and III).

A radical change came after the destruction of the second Jewish State (70 A.D.). To assure the survival of the Jewish group now under constant threat, Jewish rabbinical leadership insisted on internal unity and became intolerant of sectarianism. At the same time Christianity was becoming a purely Gentile movement, numbering more non-Jews than Jews. By the second century there was a definite movement to exclude from Christian circles the same marginal Judeo-Christians whom the Jewish people had excluded from their own ranks. In place of salvation through membership in a Jewish-Christian religious society envisaged by Peter, individual salvation through the resurrected Christ became the major emphasis of Christianity. This marked its separation from Judaism. Only thereafter did Christianity become definitely anti-Jewish. This antagonism increased as Christianity attempted to prove itself superior to Judaism in their competition with each other to win converts. The competition was real and continued up to the time when Christianity was recognized by Constantine as the State religion.

To counteract the attraction of Judaism, Christian spokesmen claimed that Christianity was the true spiritual Israel referred to in God's "Promise." To prove this claim they demonstrated that the physical Israel had been rejected. The political misfortunes of the Jews following the destruction of their State seemed to confirm their contention that God was displeased with the Jews. They, then, added further "proof" by exaggerating Jesus' criticisms of his fellow-Jews; by inventing imaginary charges including the sole guilt of the Jewish people as a whole for the crucifixion of Jesus for which all Jews must forever suffer the eternal damnation of Cain; by reviving the old fantastic attacks of pre-Christian pagans who out of sheer ignorance had accused the Jews of the strangest customs and who, because Judaism prohibited idol- and Emperor-worship, even described the Jews as being atheists! (Grayzel, 1942, pp. 25-45.)

An example of such fanatical polemics was the identification of the Jew as the actual partner of a real Devil. A single metaphor in John (John 8:44) was transformed into a realistic concept by which Christians were able to justify attacks on the Jews as attacks on Satan himself. In his *The Devil and the Jews: The Medieval Conception of the Jew and Its Relation to Modern Anti-Semitism*, Joshua Trachtenberg writes: "The most vivid impression to be gained from a reading of medieval allusions to the Jew is of a hatred so vast and abysmal, so intense, that it leaves one gasping for comprehension. The unending piling up of vile epithets and accusations and curses, the consistent representation of the Jew as the epitome of everything evil and abominable, for whom in particular the unbounded scorn and contumely of the Christian world were reserved must convince the most casual student that we are dealing here with a fanaticism altogether subjective and nonrational" (Trachtenberg, 1943, p. 12).

This popular religious stereotype, built up over a period of many centuries of Christian indoctrination, was not completely dissipated even by the liberal elements in the cultural Renaissance and the religious Reformation, by the intellectual enlightenment of the 18th century, or by the political liberalism of the 19th century. The beginning of the 20th century not only witnessed in Eastern Europe pogroms blessed with religious sanction and in Western Europe the alliance of clerics with anti-Semites in the Dreyfus affair, but also saw in America even the resurrection of the medieval charge of ritual murder against a Jew (Valentin, 1940).

The unfavorable emotional attachments to the word "Jew" built up by this long historical conflict between Christianity and Judaism has almost made it impossible for Christians to classify the modern Jew in such comparatively simple categories as nation, race, or even just another religion. Carl Mayer writes: "The impression has always prevailed that there is something strange, uncanny, and therefore incomprehensible connected with the existence of the Jews" (Graeber and Britt, 1942, p. 319). The complex social structure of the Jewish group itself does not permit a simple classification; but the so-called "mystery" about the group is inherent in the historical relation of the *religion* of the Jews to the *religion* of Christians. From this religious relationship are derived the major evaluative and emotional tones of the Jewish stereotype.

Modern studies tend to differentiate medieval anti-Semitism from modern anti-Semitism by assuming that the former was religious while the latter is racial. The religious implications are minimized because while the medieval Jew could escape persecution through baptism, the modern Jew under Nazism could not. However, it can be demonstrated that though present-day anti-Semitism is rationalized by a pseudo science of race, it grows out of the real juxtaposition of the Jewish religion to Christian society. One of the striking features of the Jewish religion is its emphasis on a distinct set of ceremonial practices based on a special calendar, customs, diet, folkways, and opposition to intermarriage. These cult practices of Judaism establish a distinct behavioral pattern. Despite the weight of scientific fact that there is no Jewish race, it is the existence of this contrasting Jewish religious behavior pattern which enabled the "racists" to put the Jew in a racial category! Religion and race become fused, and as E. Faris points out: "From the standpoint of sociology, a race is not one which is anthropologically different or biologically demonstrated. A race with which people are in conflict is a group of people *who are considered as a race* and these thoughts or considerations are determinative in conduct and in attitude" (Faris, 1935). Religious differences become the ground for racial suppositions.

On the other hand, while the "racists" exploited the religious cult differences, it is this same modern racial attack on the Jews which has served to focus attention once again on the religious values which Christianity and Judaism originally shared in common. Nazi racialism revealed itself to be an attack on the religion of Christianity as well as on the Jew. Nazi ideology claimed both democracy and Christianity to be evil deceits invented by the diabolic Jew to subdue Aryan power. The abstractions of the modern German intellectual anti-Semites were given philosophic pres-

tige by the writings of Nietzsche. The actual relationship between
Christianity and Judaism was exploited and both were declared to
be "slave morality" dangerous to the State of the racially superior
Supermen who should be "beyond good and evil." Through a
"transvaluation of values," the virile Teuton would cleanse himself of that Jewish infection, Christianity. Christian ethics were
denounced for having lowered the Aryan's resistance to the "Jewish vices," like mercy, equality, and peace, which were unmanning
the Superman.

Nazi anti-Semitism changed from a subtle strategy into an open
move to abolish Christianity. Therefore, the defense of the Jew
was made synonymous with the defense of Christianity against the
Nazi threat. As a result, haters of Jews came to be identified as
haters of Christ by modern Christian writers as well as by Jewish
writers. The Catholic philosopher, Jacques Maritain, in 1939
warned of the common fate of Jew and Christianity in a Nazi
world in his essay "A Christian Looks at the Jewish Question."
Maritain quoted these words of Pope Pius XI, when commenting
in September 1938 on the Canon of the Mass, "sacrificium patri-
archae nostri Abrahae," the Pope said: "Anti-Semitism is incompatible with the thought and sublime reality expressed in the text.
It is a movement in which we Christians can have no part whatsoever. . . . Anti-Semitism is unacceptable. Spiritually we are
Semites" (Maritain, 1939, p. 41). The Jewish publicist, Maurice
Samuel in *The Great Hatred* (1940) popularized the challenge
to Christianity implicit in Naziism, declaring the latter's recourse
to anti-Semitism to be "not a confusion at all, but the right mental
strategy of those who hate and fear Christ" (Samuel, 1940, p. 36).
The public action of Nazi anti-Christians gave substance to these
Christian and Jewish charges. They abolished the Old Testament,
rewrote the Sermon on the Mount to remove from it the "Jewish
influences," namely its emphasis on peace and humility, and taught
Hitler youth to sing: "Pope and Rabbi shall be gone. We want to
be pagan once again. No more creep to Churches."

In view of the threat of an amoral neo-barbarism to Christianity and Judaism alike, an ideologic change has been taking place in the intellectual approach of many present-day Christian spokesmen toward Jews. When they speak of anti-Semitism they no longer refer to it as the "Jewish Problem" but as the "Christian Problem." The "Judeo-Christian heritage" is now frequently referred to as the basis of Western civilization and the hope of a free and moral society. In Christian circles considerable attention is given to elements in Christian doctrine which stimulate anti-Jewish feelings in Christians. Recently, the Sacred Congregation of Rites declared in an official organ of the Vatican Curia that the Latin expressions "Perfidi Iudaei" and "Iudaica Perfidia" used in Good Friday homilies should no longer be translated in any vernacular as "perfidious Jews" and "Jewish perfidy" with the usual connotations that the Jews are guilty of fraud and treachery. "This Sacred Congregation, having been consulted about the matter, has deemed it advisable to make the following declaration only: that, in translations into the vernacular, phrases are not disapproved of which the meaning is: "wanting in (Christian) belief (infidelitas, infideles incredendo)" (American Jewish Committee, 1949). Liberal elements in the Protestant Church have gone further in this area by reinterpreting and revaluating the Crucifixion story and the Pharisees; by investigating and eliminating anti-Jewish attitudes in Sunday School textbooks; and by joining with Jewish religious organizations for the purpose of furthering brotherhood.

Two approaches may be observed in this effort to reduce anti-Jewish attitudes within the religious frame of reference. One is the conscious recognition on the part of Christian leadership of the positive rather than the negative historical affinity between Christianity and Judaism. The other is the new emphasis on the fact that both religions hold many religious values in common. Both approaches are generally subsumed under "Jewish Contributions to Christianity" which includes Jesus, the Bible, divine cosmology, absolutistic ethics, democratic polity, social meliorism, pacifism, and such institutions as the Sabbath and the Church. It is assumed that knowledge of Christianity's dependence on Judaism together with an appreciation of the values both religions hold in common will reduce anti-Jewish attitudes. Furthermore, there is in Christianity an emotional emphasis on the ethics of love. It would follow that this brotherly attitude would be directed also to the Jew, especially after the Christian would realize how much he is indebted to the Jew's ancestors for this equalitarian morality. However, it has never been proven by psychological tests whether emotional preachment directing Christian love specifically toward Jews or whether informing the Christian of the Jew's contributions to Christianity or whether both combined do appreciably change anti-Jewish attitudes, to say nothing of anti-Jewish behavior.

A program of intercultural education which teaches the Jewish contributions to the Christian doctrine of loving one's neighbor might conceivably increase resentment against Jews. Lewin and Grabbe observe that "reeducation is frequently in danger of reaching only the official system of values, the level of verbal expression and not of conduct; it may result in merely heightening the discrepancy between the superego (the way I ought to feel) and the ego (the way I really feel) and thus give the individual a bad conscience. Such a discrepancy leads to a state of high emotional tension but seldom to correct conduct" (Lewin and Grabbe, 1945, p. 59).

The psychoanalytic approach to anti-Semitism makes a strong argument of this assumption. In reducing anti-Semitic attitudes, "should there simply be an appeal for fair play, to a sense of justice in the individual, to the ideals of democracy?" asks Max Horkheimer, and his answer is: "The psychoanalytic answer would be in the negative. A mere appeal to the conscious mind does not suffice because anti-Semitism and the susceptibility to anti-Semitic propaganda spring from the unconscious" (Simmel, 1946, p. 2).

Anti-Semitism as a subconscious mechanism has two hypotheses, the one highly metaphysical, the other functional, and both are rooted in religious concepts. Grafting the theory of the Oedipus complex upon a questionable Biblical exegesis, Sigmund Freud in *Moses and Monotheism* speculated that Christians have been unable to resolve the atavistic guilt of father-murder common to the whole human race before organized religion (Freud, 1939). Christians are resentful of the Jews whose religion enabled them to achieve a workable resolution of this universal primitive crime. According to Freud, the symbol of Jesus on the Cross constantly stimulates in Christians an unconscious memory of this guilt for the murder of the father. Judaism has no such symbolic reminder. In fact, one of its rites, the rite of circumcision, is, according to one psychoanalytic theory, an atonement offering that propitiates the God-Father and thus resolves for the Jew man's unconscious fear of castration which is supposed to be the punishment for father-murder.

The Christian may try to escape his own primitive guilt of father-murder and the symbolization of it in the crucifix, says Freud, by turning to the legend that it was the "Jews who killed Christ," who was himself a Jew. By this charge the Christian can project his own unresolved primitive guilt feelings on to the Jew. According to psychoanalytic theory making the Christian more conscious of Jewish contributions to Christianity could act as a "boomerang" and reinforce anti-Semitism.

This Freudian theory is highly metaphysical. On the other hand, the actual association of anti-Semitism with the Nazi revolt against Christianity and the Nazi return to paganism gives some substance to a functional analysis of anti-Semitism as a subconscious rebellion against the moral restraints of Christianity. According to this point of view, it is less the fact that the Jews are charged with the murder of Christ than the fact that Christ was himself a Jew which gives rise to anti-Jewish feelings. Christian authority prohibits sensual indulgence which, therefore, must be repressed and at the same time it sets altruistic goals, like "turning the other cheek," which are most difficult to attain. Such a situation engenders frustration; these feelings are relieved by aggression. Since conscious aggression against Christ as the frustrating object is inadmissible in Christian society, it can be transferred to the Jews through Christ's identification with them. Therefore, the more one identifies Christianity with the Jews the more could Jews become the object of Christian hostility. This theory might be tested by measuring whether the anti-Jewish attitude is actually increased by teaching the Christian about Jewish contributions to Christianity.

Psychoanalysis doubts that a Christian anti-Semite will change his attitude toward the Jews when he learns that the Jewish religion is the basis of his acquired Christian conscience, a conscience which he subconsciously resents. Psychoanalysis challenges the effectiveness of interfaith programs designed to awaken the Christian conscience of anti-Semites.

Recent studies of the character structure of the bigoted personality undertaken by the University of California Public Opinion Study seem to support this criticism. By use of the Levinson-Sanford Scale for measuring anti-Semitism, the most anti-Semitic subjects and the least anti-Semitic subjects were determined in this investigation. By personal interviews and by such projective techniques as the Rorschach and Murray Thematic Apperception Tests, detailed studies were made of the most anti-Semitic subjects. It was shown that unconscious layers of sadistic impulses, unsatisfied sexual desires, intense anxiety about their middle class social status, suspicions about unknown life forces and inner conflict with puritanical and tyrannical parents lay beneath the exterior conventional morality of these most anti-Semitic students. Their prejudice against Jews results not only from the ethnocentrism of their class membership but functions as a needed dynamism in their personalities for the release of repressed hostility. "Basic impulses which are conceived as low, destructive, and dangerous have to be kept repressed and can find only devious expressions as, for instance, in projections and 'moral indignation.' Thus, anti-Semitism and intolerance against out-groups generally may have an important function in keeping the personality integrated. Without these channels or outlets . . . it may be much more difficult, in some cases impossible, to keep the mental balances. Hence, the rigid and compulsive adherence to prejudices" (Frenkel and Sanford, 1945; Simmel, 1946, p. 117).

It not only appears futile to the psychoanalyst to activate the Christian conscience of the psychopathological person, it may even heighten his emotional conflict and increase irrational hostility. Yet, as Gordon W. Allport suggests, "May it not be that *most* people (not, of course, the paranoid type of bigot) have a sufficiently strong ego structure to resist the depredations of anti-Semitism if, as decent and democratic citizens, they are warned of its perils and its insidious modes of operation? As a critic of psychoanalysis I have often thought (and sometimes written) that psychoanalytic theory tends to ascribe to *all* mortals the same type of subservience to unconscious hostilities and fixations that unquestionably mark the mental life of neurotics and psychotics. I know that the reply to my criticism is that *degrees* of unconscious fixation exist in all people. But even if this is so, it seems to me that conscious sentiments of decency, compassion and *fidelity to religious faith* [italics mine] are often sufficiently dynamic to control the prejudice" (Simmel, 1946, p. vii).

THE INDIRECT GROUP METHOD

May we assume that the emotional appeal which the Christian religion makes in behalf of brotherhood does reduce the prejudices of less fixated persons whose hostility against Jews is not so profoundly irrational? May we also assume that a knowledge of the Jewish origins of his faith will help this Christian change whatever anti-Jewish attitudes he holds? In a pagan society in which Christian values had not yet taken root, the writings of a Josephus about Jewish contributions to civilization might have little appeal. Such a cultural defense of the Jew could not counteract the anti-Semitic prejudices of an Apione, a Cicero, or a Tacitus partly because in pagan cultures there was no general emotional receptivity for the religious and moral values in Judaism whose superiority Josephus had advocated. However, would not centuries of indoctrination in the Christian religious sentiments derived from Judaism create an altogether different cultural climate within which

"Jewish contributions" might become more readily recognizable?

Furthermore, teaching the factual relation of Christianity to Judaism and their common basis in the Bible could carry emotional influence as well as information because of the inherent evaluative and qualitative nature of religion to the religious. In Christian culture and particularly in Church circles, the Bible is not a factual book dealing with Jewish antiquity but a divine revelation. For this reason, the Bible has an emotional influence which extends from the Sunday School nursery to the oath-taking ceremonies of the President of the United States. The phrase "The Bible" is a synonym for the "good life." The very word "Bible" is a powerful semantic directive which is supposed to point out to the individual the way to ethical relationships as well as to cosmic salvation. Furthermore, when the Bible is taught in religious institutions, it enjoys the prestige of the "sacred" authority of those institutions. Thus, in Christian religious groups, the Bible has more than historical and literary interest; it has an unequalled emotional valence.

The term "valence" is used by Kurt Lewin to describe the "affective property" of material which possesses "value judgments." Muzafer Sherif has demonstrated that the emotional valence of a judgment-fact may have a negative or positive reaction on a prejudice, depending on its use (Sherif, 1936). In other words, the attitude of a Christian toward a Jew within an influential religious frame of reference may be changed by proper use of the "valence" of the Biblical material.

If teaching the Bible in Christian circles as a Jewish contribution were only informational without any such emotional effect, the instruction could not be expected to change anti-Jewish prejudice. Most psychological studies have demonstrated that factual information alone has little, if any, effect in reducing prejudice. An examination and classification of this field of research was made by Arnold Rose (Rose, 1947) and Robin M. Williams, Jr. (Williams, 1947). Their summaries reveal that the presentation of objective facts about groups results in no favorable changes or only inconclusive ones, though no important changes in a more prejudiced direction have been reported. In his recent book *The More Perfect Union,* dealing with controls of inter-group discrimination, R. M. MacIver includes an appendix on the effect of information on attitudes. Prepared by Robert Bierstedt, this survey of the research confirms the low correlation between a knowledge of favorable facts about a group and tolerance for that group (MacIver, 1948, pp. 288–302). *Information does not reduce prejudice.*

Most of the research in the field of changing prejudices has dealt with Negro-White relations. In an early study on "Some Effects of a Course in American Race Problems on the Race Prejudice of 450 Undergraduates at the University of Pennsylvania," the students, before and after the course, were asked to rank a list of 20 races and nationalities according to their "inborn ability" starting with number one as the highest. Despite the course, which disproved "inborn racial ability," there was no improvement in attitudes. As for attitude toward Jews, Group I ranked Jews 7.0 before and 8.5 after the course, while Group II ranked Jews 7.0 before and 11.5 after. Here the results showed slightly more prejudice toward the Jews after the course than before. Donald Young, the investigator, observed that the general results were "startling in that they were monotonously unchanged" and that they "raise the question of the efficiency of a teaching method which is essentially a logical presentation of the facts and theories" (Young, 1927).

On the other hand, many studies have shown that the unconditioning of hostility can be effective if techniques are used which contain: an emotional appeal (Chen, 1933; Cherrington, 1934; Hartman, 1936; Peterson and Thurstone, 1933); prestige symbols (Kulp, 1934; Lorge, 1935; Saadi and Fransworth, 1934; Sorokin and Boldgreff, 1932); or include friendly contact between the ingroup and an out-group of equal cultural and economic status (Campbell and Stover, 1933; Smith, 1943). Harlan reports that less frequent but greater intimacy of contact is related to more favorable attitudes toward Jews (Harlan, 1942). If, to information per se are added these three dimensions for influencing attitudes—

emotional appeal, prestige symbols and equal status, friendly contact, it would appear that anti-Jewish attitudes within a Christian religious setting might be changed.

This four-dimensional method is now being employed in Christian-Jewish interfaith education. For the express purpose of improving intergroup relations, Rabbis are frequently invited to teach Bible and impart information on Judaism to Christians. The stimulus material employed—the Bible—has inherent emotional value to Christians and may be used to effect changes in their attitudes. Authorized by the Church to teach in the environment of the Church itself, the Rabbi is given prestige. Through his development of friendly associations with the Christian students, the rabbinical representative of the Jewish minority is able to establish equal status contact with the Christian majority. In this favorable situation, the information presented by the Rabbi includes the Jewish historical origins and the Jewish theological foundations of Christianity, as well as an emphasis on those Biblical religious values which Jew and Christian share in common. Do these advantages of emotional appeal, prestige, and association counterbalance the deeper psychological resistance which, nonetheless, may be aroused in the Christian by this information?

In view of the actual historical conflict between Christianity and Judaism, and in view of the suggested subconscious anti-Jewish hostility which may be aggravated by a conscious knowledge of the Jewish origins of Christianity, this four-dimensional method might conceivably *increase* anti-Jewish attitudes. The effectiveness of this intercultural approach has never been examined. The purpose of our study is to test its results. We shall call this method the Indirect Group Method, because it does not include any direct discussion of specific anti-Jewish attitudes. No references are made to contemporary prejudices against Jews by the instructor, nor are the students encouraged to speak of their own attitudes toward Jews or of their personal experiences with Jews.

Opportunity to test the Indirect Group Method experimentally was afforded the writer, who is a Rabbi, when he was invited by two Protestant denominations to teach the Old Testament to their high school students. This age level is probably more readily influenced than older groups, because of the religious doubting that begins in this adolescent period (Kuhlen and Arnold, 1944) and because the attitudes of this age group are less set than older groups (Gardner, 1935). At the same time, it is a critical period for the formation of anti-Jewish feelings as a compensation for adolescent frustrations. Allport reports that half of the college students in his study indicated that their dislike for Jews began between the ages of 12 and 16 (Allport and Kramer, 1946).

Through the auspices of the Jewish Chautauqua Society (an organization sponsored by the National Federation of Temple Brotherhoods to create better understanding by promulgating information about Judaism in academic circles), the Rabbi was invited by the Departments of Religious Education of the Episcopal Diocese of the State of Connecticut, and by the national office of the Methodist Church of America, to participate in a series of their Summer Camp Seminars. The Episcopal Seminars were held in Connecticut in the summer of 1946, and the Methodist Seminars were held in West Virginia in the summer of 1947. Five hundred and twenty-five students participated in these Church Camp Seminars. In this study, 357 of these students comprised a control group, and 168 students the experimental group. Seventy of the latter were subjects of the Indirect Group Method.

THE DIRECT GROUP METHOD

We have assumed that the Indirect Group Method might not decrease anti-Jewish attitudes. On theoretical grounds, it might even increase prejudice. We have also observed that the Indirect Group Method does not deal directly with anti-Jewish feelings. Recent experimental studies in the general field of changing attitudes have shown that, whereas information is ineffective, the technique of verbal catharsis and the active participation of a group in an issue is productive of favorable changes in attitude.

Gordon Allport states in his article, "Catharsis and the Reduction of Prejudice" (Allport, 1945); "Everyone knows that straight lectures on the interests, rights and virtues of minority groups accomplish very little. The listener is often so near to bursting with hostility that nothing new can come into his mind until something old comes out . . . retrainers who encounter more resistance than they expect may need to provide more abundantly for the free expression of hostility." Such expression may serve either as a "complacency shock" or a talking cure. Of course, this catharsis must be guided or "it may merely reinforce all the disordered tendencies" and "freeze the self-justifications and projections." Allport concludes that "the cathartic process has led his listeners to admit some guilt even while evading some, or to shock themselves out of their complacency or to exhaust their pent up hostility until they are receptive to new facts and new points of view. It is only then that the reconstructing of attitudes begins."

The extensive investigations of Kurt Lewin point to two important considerations for an effective modification of attitudes: one, the individual must become actively involved in the problem and two, the individual more readily accepts those new values if he believes them to be accepted by the group in which he belongs. This hypothesis suggests the effectiveness of the in-group's open, but guided, discussion and evaluation of its own hostility against an out-group in the light of the in-group's own moral and religious values. Furthermore "by anchoring his own conduct in something as large, substantial and supra-individual as the culture of a group, can the individual stabilize his new beliefs sufficiently to keep them immune from the day-by-day fluctuations of mood and influences" (Lewin and Grabbe, 1945, p. 54). Group investigation of its own stereotype thinking and group decisions about the validity of such prejudgments will tend to diminish the prejudice of individual members in the group (Lewin, 1943 and 1944).

Verbal catharsis could be applied in changing anti-Jewish attitudes by providing opportunity for the students of a Christian group to express their attitudes toward Jews, pro and con. The members of the group might become actively involved in the problem of prejudice against the Jew by the group's direct discussion of the contemporary Christian-Jewish issue.

The method which employs the cathartic process through the dynamic participation of the group and the instructor in the direct expression and evaluation of the group's hostility toward Jews will be referred to here as the Direct Group Method. In this study in the Indirect and the Direct Group Method the same four-dimensional approach and the same Biblical materials and information on common ideals and Jewish contributions to Christianity are used. In the Direct Group Method, however, they serve as a springboard for a direct group discussion of contemporary anti-Jewish attitudes. Seventy-three students of the experimental groups of the Episcopalian and of the Methodist Seminars were the subjects of the Direct Group Method to test its effectiveness in changing anti-Jewish attitudes.

Since emotional influences are involved in the Direct Method as well as in the Indirect Method for changing anti-Jewish attitude, testing the difference between the results of the two methods, is not just a test of whether a "factual" approach is less or more effective than an "emotional" appeal. We are here comparing complex types of instruction rather than single techniques. In general terms the issue is that of the differential consequences of direct approaches as against indirect, nonmanifest methods of influencing group relations. Theodore Brameld states that the opinion of educators ranges from the belief that "the best way to handle intergroup relations is to say as little as possible about them" to the policy of singling out an intergroup tension for explicit attention (Brameld, 1946). The observation of Robin M. Williams, Jr. in this matter is worth noting. He says: "Probably no other question of approach in this field has been more extensively—and heatedly—discussed than this. For all its vigor, the discussion has failed to produce definite conclusions or even an appreciable consensus of opinion. The only reasonably certain point is that no clear answer of 'good' or 'bad' can be expected when the question is raised in general terms. What is needed first of all is a series of repetitive studies to determine the concomitants of particular actions, based upon assumptions at one pole or the other. Only when these studies are complete can we hope to arrive at verified general conclusions" (Williams, 1947). It is hoped that this experiment, which will analyze the results of the indirect as compared to the direct approach for reducing anti-Jewish prejudice, will make some contribution to the general science of improving intergroup relations.

THE FOCUSED PRIVATE INTERVIEW

In addition to the Indirect and Direct Group Methods, a third method for changing attitudes was examined in this investigation. The Methodist Seminar permitted an experiment with three equated groups: one was taught by the Indirect Method, another by the Direct Method and a third by the Focused Private Interview. In the class, the third group was taught by the Indirect Method but each member of the class was given a thirty minute private interview with the Rabbi. In this personal conference, the interview was focused on the students' own experiences with Jews, on the specific subject of Christian attitudes toward Jews and on a discussion of what can be done about Christian-Jewish relations. A questionnaire with a definite fixed set of questions was not used. While some of the non-directive techniques were employed, the main purpose was to "focus" attention on the problem while allowing the respondent freedom to pursue his own associations. This interview technique is described by Merton and Kendall (Merton and Kendall, 1946).

Previous studies have demonstrated the factor of "interviewer bias" according to which the group membership of the interviewer, as indicated by color, name, or even less obvious characteristics of the interviewer having no relation to group membership, will significantly affect the answers of the respondents. Robinson and Rohde show that in their poll on anti-Semitism the "Jewishness" or the "non-Jewishness" of the interviewer affected the replies

(Robinson and Rohde, 1945). Obviously there can be no mistaking the group membership of the interviewer in this study, but if bias appears in the Focused Private Interview Method, the same bias appears in the other two methods with which it will be compared since it is the same Rabbi in each situation.

Unlike poll-taking, the interviews here were not for the purpose of gathering information but for the purpose of affecting a change in attitude. While they seem to collect information, the interviews intend to involve the individual directly and consciously in the Christian-Jewish problem. The individual is encouraged to relate his own experiences. He frequently projects his own attitudes in the statements he attributes to other Christians. Effort is made to reorient the individual's thinking when his misinformation or prejudice calls for it. To a certain extent, the Focused Private Interview is the Direct Group Method of this study applied privately to the individual for the purpose of getting him personally involved, and to bring about catharsis. Twenty-five students in the Methodist experimental group participated in the Focused Private Interview.

THE EXPERIMENTAL DESIGN

In the Episcopal Connecticut Seminar, only the Indirect and Direct Group methods were used, for only two groups, numbering 49 and 48 students each were available for the experiment. Three separate groups, numbering 163, 149, and 116 students each, attended the Methodist West Virginia Seminar which made it possible to introduce there the Focused Private Interview in addition to the Indirect and Direct Group Methods. Each group remained one full week at the seminars, and then returned home to make room for the next group. Students attending the Episcopal Seminar came from all parts of Connecticut, from small rural towns and large cities representing various parishes. The students at the Methodist Seminar gathered together from towns and cities of West Virginia, representing various churches. They came from all economic strata: from the homes of farmers, skilled and unskilled laborers, business men, professionals, bankers, industrialists, the middle class and the upper class.

The students enjoyed the friendly atmosphere of a summer recreational camp, and at the same time, they were surrounded by a definite religious environment. Both the Episcopalian and the Methodist Seminars included public prayer, hymn singing, daily Chapel attendance, communion services and special courses on the creed, the cult and the conduct of the respective denominations. The purpose, as stated in the brochures of each Seminar, was to develop not only Christian lay leadership but to encourage students to enter the ministry or other avenues of Christian endeavor such as social welfare and education. Members of the faculties were clergymen and professional leaders of the Episcopal Church and the Methodist Church respectively. The only exception was the Rabbi. The Rabbi attended all functions at the camps, including attendance as a visitor at religious services. He participated in the recreational program and lived in the dormitories with the students and faculty. The course he taught at the Episcopal Seminar was "The Psalms" and at the Methodist Seminar, "The Old Testament in the Life of Today." Stenographic reports were recorded for all sessions.

In the design of this experiment, the problems of sampling, the personality variance of the instructor, the equating of the groups, and a scale for measuring attitudes toward Jews presented complex methodological problems. Inasmuch as the instructor was the same Rabbi in every situation, this variable was adequately controlled. However, in the equation of the groups, we did not have the rather rigorous control available in the formally organized public school class where it is possible to match experimental and control groups for "before and after testing" of the effect of a single variable change in the instruction. This advantage for an experimental design may be offset by the artificiality of a school population. In this study we have an ex post facto experiment. We accept the "natural" groups available without precise control of individual factors. Effort was made to equate factors of intelligence, sex, age, economic status, and residence to determine in what major respects, if any, one group may differ enough from the other to affect the stability of the inferences drawn. Furthermore, for a closer approximation of control, the results of the various methods were compared on the basis of selected cases from each group matched for initial scores in the attitudes scale.

A scale for measuring attitudes toward Jews was prepared and administered to each group before and after the course of studies. The scale was filled out anonymously. Furthermore, it was neither administered by the Rabbi nor filled out in the Rabbi's class. In each situation the Deans of the Seminars distributed the attitudes scale to the entire student body at an assembly which the Rabbi did not attend and before any student had met the Rabbi. The Dean stated that the Seminar was asked to cooperate with a group of psychologists making a study of the attitudes of groups in America toward each other. The students were told not to sign their names and were asked to check the questionnaire as honestly as possible. The post-test taken one week later, also in a general assembly not attended by the Rabbi, was explained by the Deans as a usual technique in such public opinion surveys which repeat the questionnaire for a recheck and it was requested that the students just check once more how they felt about the questions asked. Thus, effort was made to disassociate the course of studies with the Rabbi from the administration of the attitudes scale. The contents of the scale for measuring anti-Jewish attitudes will now be described.

II. A SCALE FOR MEASURING

ATTITUDE TOWARD THE JEW

A SCALE containing sixteen statements to estimate the attitude of an individual toward Jews was prepared. It is based on recent investigations regarding scaling techniques (McNemar, 1946). The Likert simple scoring method is used (Likert, 1932). The marking system is the conventional four-point type which requires the subject to indicate "agreement," "slight agreement," "slight disagreement," or "disagreement" with each statement. In the tabulation, o is awarded to the least prejudiced response, 3 to the most prejudiced, and 1 and 2 to the intermediate responses. The "don't know" category which tends to be an avoidance-reaction, is omitted. The total score range for the sixteen items is o to 48. Low scores indicate the rejection of anti-Jewish attitudes and high scores the acceptance of anti-Jewish attitudes.

The items in the scale are selected from the *opinions* that non-Jews may have of what Jews are supposed to be like and of what Jews are expected to do. Certain items are derived from the *attitudes* that non-Jews may have regarding what they should do for or against Jews. The scale includes such typical prejudiced stereotypes and social expectancy as the so-called money power of the Jew, his clannishness, his aggressiveness, his avoidance of hard work; it questions his patriotism, his effect on places of residence, his role in government; and it suggests the restriction of the Jew in employment and colleges, opposition to intermarriage with

Jews, and it questions Christian defense of the Jew (see Table 1).

Thirteen of the sixteen items are closely related to similar statements in "A Scale for the Measurement of Anti-Semitism" constructed by Levinson and Sanford (Levinson and Sanford, 1944), in which the above mentioned distinction between opinion and attitude is made. Allport and Kramer chose the most discriminatory items in the Levinson-Sanford scale for the eight statements regarding Jews in their general minority attitudes scale (Allport and Kramer, 1946). In the present scale, preference is also given to the most discriminatory items in the Levinson-Sanford scale. However, because of their popular contemporary role in attitudes toward Jews, a number of items are included in the scale of this study despite their lower discriminatory power as reported in the Levinson-Sanford study. For example, the item "Colleges should adopt a quota system by which they limit the number of Jews in fields which have too many Jews now" ranks 37th in discriminatory power in the Levinson-Sanford study. The elimination of this item on the results of a statistical analysis of their small sampling of 77 cases confined to college students is unwarranted. On the other hand, to prefer the item "It is best that Jews should have their own fraternities and sororities, etc.," because it ranks first in discriminatory power is also to overlook the fact that the Levinson-Sanford sample is localized to a college student population where this particular item receives primary personal interest. The "pro" and "anti" evaluation of test items is conditioned by the frame of reference in which they are presented (Kay, 1947).

A conceptual distinction should be made between the Levinson-Sanford scale and the scale constructed for this study. Levinson and Sanford specifically describe their questionnaire as a scale to measure anti-Semitism, stating that it measures the degree of the individual's readiness to support or oppose "active anti-Semitism." In order to present "the total content of anti-Semitic ideology," their excessively long scale of 52 items includes statements on economic, political, religious, cultural, social, and personal matters in which hostile attitudes toward Jews have been expressed. An effort is made to expose the irrationality of anti-Semitism by giving the respondent the opportunity to react to contradictory statements such as accusing the Jew of being exclusive while at the same time criticizing him if he tries to assimilate. To tap these inconsistencies in the thought pattern of anti-Semitism, 28 of the 52 items were expressly prepared by the pairing of such contradictory statements. Furthermore, all statements in the Levinson-Sanford scale are in the negative or are hostile toward the Jews in order to invite a response to "active anti-Semitism."

The scale in the present study is *not* a measurement of anti-Semitism. It measures the tendency of the individual to agree or disagree with anti-Jewish or pro-Jewish verbal statements. It presents a score in prejudice toward Jews.

Anti-Semitism differs from an anti-Jewish attitude in definiteness and intensity. In anti-Semitism one finds a positive even though irrational body of racist ideas according to which the Jews are the cause of all social ills. From this ideology is derived a consistent policy which calls for the suppression of the Jews to cure these ills. Anti-Semitism then transforms this policy into an active propaganda and an organized movement for power.

An anti-Jewish attitude is not based on any such complete ideologic pattern nor is it necessarily activated. It may vary in intensity, but an anti-Jewish attitude is more like the group prejudice that exists between many other unlike social groups. Anti-Semites try to exploit and organize these less definitive anti-Jewish attitudes. An anti-Semite with psychopathic obsessions may never change his fixed pathological attitude; but one who is anti-Jewish may change his attitude. The latter may become more or less prejudiced depending on the factor of influence.

Three items which have no counterpart in the Levinson-Sanford scale are included in the scale of this study. Item 16, "One can tell whether a person he meets is Jewish," plays an important role in the average relationship of Jew and non-Jew. Allport and Kramer report a positive correlation between those with higher anti-Jewish scores and the ability of these more prejudiced to judge correctly which were the "Jewish faces" in a "racial awareness" experiment with photographs of Jews and non-Jews. It seems that the unprejudiced is less sensitive than the bigot to the identity of those with whom he deals (Allport and Kramer, 1946).

Item 10, "People who are not Jewish should try to answer those who say things against Jews" brings out another general experience in Jew and non-Jew relationships. It refers to the prevalence of "the anti-Jewish remark" as well as more vehement charges. The statement is relevant to that part of this study which will test the behavior changes, if any, in this particular area as a result of change in attitudes.

Item 14, "We are indebted to the Jews for their contribution to religion," applies directly to the stimulus material in this study which deals with the question of whether acknowledgement of the Judaic origins of Christian belief will decrease the degree of anti-Jewish attitude. Items 17 and 18 are informational. They are not scored but are used for other validational purposes.

The scale of Form A as it was presented to the subjects is given in Table 1. Form A comprised the initial test. To reduce the factor of mental set, the title "A Scale for Measuring Attitude toward the Jew" did not appear on the form.

Form B (see Appendix A) of this scale was used for the post-test. The items of Form B are identical with those of Form A. However, they are presented in a different order and in the form of direct questions. As will be observed in a comparison of the initial test and the post-test one week later of 309 respondents who received no intervening instruction, the subjects tend to give slightly higher mean scores in Form B (that is, indicating more prejudice). In Form A, this group has a mean of 17.5 and a standard deviation of 8.67; in Form B it has a mean of 18.67 and a standard deviation of 9.75. The standard error of the difference is 4.2. While statistically there is a significant difference, practically it is only a difference of one item in the mean score. However, the standard deviation of Form B is greater than that of Form A, and therefore Form B achieves greater discrimination within the group. The

TABLE I

A SCALE FOR MEASURING ATTITUDE TOWARD THE JEW

Form A

DO NOT WRITE YOUR NAME ON THIS PAPER   PLEASE FILL IN ALL BLANKS

BOY_____GIRL_____   Do you live in a town?_____large city?_____

What school grade are you in now? _____ Birth date _____

What work does your father do? _____

THIS IS NOT A TEST. THERE ARE NO "RIGHT" OR "WRONG" ANSWERS. Check the column which shows how *you feel* about each statement. Your name is not asked for. Be as straightforward as you can.

	I agree	I slightly agree	I slightly disagree	I disagree
1. Jews control too much of the wealth of this country.	_____	_____	_____	_____
2. When Jews move into a nice section they spoil the neighborhood.	_____	_____	_____	_____
3. Jews did their fair share in the war.	_____	_____	_____	_____
4. Anyone who employs many people should be careful not to hire too many Jews.	_____	_____	_____	_____
5. Jews play a valuable part in American life.	_____	_____	_____	_____
6. With a few exceptions, Jews are pretty much alike.	_____	_____	_____	_____
7. Colleges and professional schools should limit the number of Jews they admit.	_____	_____	_____	_____
8. Jews try whenever possible to get out of doing their share of any real hard work.	_____	_____	_____	_____
9. Jews live in Jewish sections of cities because they are clannish and insist on sticking together.	_____	_____	_____	_____

10. People who are not Jewish should try to answer those

	I agree	I slightly agree	I slightly disagree	I disagree
who say things against the Jews.	____	____	____	____
11. There are too many Jews in government positions.	____	____	____	____
12. It would be all right if a member of your family wanted to marry a Jewish person.	____	____	____	____
13. Jews usually try to push ahead without considering the rights of others.	____	____	____	____
14. We are indebted to the Jews for their contribution to religion.	____	____	____	____
15. Jews should have as good a chance as others to get into any kind of work.	____	____	____	____
16. One can tell whether a person he meets is Jewish.	____	____	____	____

	None	Very little	Average	Considerable
17. How much experience have you had with a Jew or Jews?	____	____	____	____

	None	1 or 2	5	10
18. Do you have any Jewish friends?	____	____	____	____

modality of the test experience in Form B tends to force more 1 and 2 responses which increases the mean score (see Table 2). This preference for intermediate responses suggests that the direct question form, "Do you think," in Form B makes the respondent less decisive than when he answers the declarative statements in Form A.

TABLE 2

THE DISTRIBUTION OF THE AVERAGES OF THE 0-1-2-3 RESPONSES (N309)

	Mean Score	S.D.	0	1	2	3
Form A	17.50	8.67	7.56	3.10	2.61	2.80
Form B	18.67	9.75	5.45	4.95	3.54	2.07

A correction chart was not deemed feasible or necessary for this study. Since post-test Form B tends to give a higher score than Form A, it follows that the ratio of the difference would be even more significant than the statistical significance of change might indicate should the post-test for the estimate of change show a lower mean score than the initial test. In other words, if a person is expected to give a higher score in Form B than in Form A but instead gives a lower score, the decrease in his anti-Jewish prejudice is that much greater.

The reliability of the scale is calculated by two methods: by the split half method of correlating the total scores of each subject on the odd and even items; and by correlating the total scores of each subject on two different forms of the questionnaire given to these subjects at one week's interval. The correlation between Form A and Form B for 309 respondents is .85. This together with the correlations of .82 to .89 according to the odd-even split half technique on Form A as recorded in Table 3 renders a satisfactory reliability for the scale.

TABLE 3

ODD-EVEN SPLIT HALF RELIABILITY

Form A

Group	N	Raw Score	Corrected
Conn. I	49	.72	.84
Conn. II	48	.81	.89
W. Va. I	102	.70	.82
W. Va. II	115	.77	.87
W. Va. III	92	.71	.83

The criterion of internal consistency, which Likert (Murphy and Likert, 1938) and Sletto (Sletto, 1937) found correlates highly with results obtained by item analysis, was applied to the scale. This criterion establishes the relatedness of each item in the scale to the total scale. Internal consistency is determined by the power of each item to discriminate between the highest quartile and the lowest quartile in the distribution of the scores. To be consistent, those subjects who get high and low scores on the total test should tend also to get high and low scores respectively on each item. An item on which those who are more anti-Jewish score lower than those who are less anti-Jewish would obviously be an item out of place in this scale. Also if the two extreme groups get about the same average score on an item, then that item fails to discriminate in the test. As will be seen in Table 4, in all of the sixteen items of Form A the higher scorers on the total test also get the higher scores on each item.

In comparison with other studies, using the criterion of internal consistency and employing scales with three- to seven-point marking range, the discriminabilities obtained in the scale of this study are relatively high. Using the same threshold of acceptability of discriminating powers as applied to a five-point marking range, namely, 0.8 to 1.0 (which could be even lower for a four-point range), all but one of the items in the present scale are acceptable. Excluding item 15, the range of discriminabilities in the Connecticut Group is 0.8 to 2.16 and in the West Virginia Group 0.91 to 2.01. Sletto states that "If the N is 200 or larger, as it ought to be to obtain reasonably stable value, the probability that a difference of 1:00 between quartile means will yield a critical ratio of 3:00 or better is sufficiently great to make calculations of such ratios unnecessary" (Sletto, 1937).

Item 15, "Jews should have as good a chance as others to get into any kind of work," seems to invite the conventional self-righteous reaction of "tolerance" or an expected affirmation of "fair-play" without stimulating much feeling on the matter, for it does not adequately distinguish the most prejudiced from the least prejudiced. Since, however, even this item was not entirely negative in discriminatory power, it was not discarded.

The reliability, the internal consistency, and the general validity of the item content justifies the use of the scale as an operational measurement of anti-Jewish or pro-Jewish attitudes.

An analysis of 479 of the 525 respondents who completed all the items in the initial tests in this study, reveals that the highest quar-

TABLE 4

AVERAGE SCORES AND DISCRIMINATORY POWERS
OF THE SCALE ITEMS IN FORM A

Connecticut Group (N97)

| ITEM | MEAN OF | | | DISCRIMINA-TORY POWER |
	Entire Group	Highest Quartile	Lowest Quartile	
1	1.18	1.96	.30	1.66
2	.82	1.75	.26	1.49
3	.71	1.19	.30	.89
4	.77	1.36	.17	1.19
5	1.06	1.54	.26	1.28
6	1.74	2.64	.48	2.16
7	.77	1.64	.00	1.64
8	.78	1.46	.04	1.42
9	1.35	1.79	.56	1.23
10	1.28	1.75	.95	.80
11	.80	1.68	.13	1.55
12	1.69	2.50	.69	1.81
13	1.55	2.43	.39	2.04
14	1.16	1.75	.61	1.14
15	.32	.54	.35	.19
16	1.21	1.86	.48	1.38

Highest Quartile, 28 cases, score range 23–42.
Lowest Quartile, 23 cases, score range 0–9.

West Virginia Group (N382)

ITEM	Entire Group	Highest Quartile	Lowest Quartile	DISCRIMINATORY POWER
1	1.21	2.11	.38	1.73
2	.40	1.03	.07	.96
3	.66	1.32	.28	1.04
4	.90	1.81	.23	1.58
5	1.02	1.93	.27	1.66
6	1.73	2.51	.92	1.59
7	.60	1.47	.06	1.41
8	.80	1.71	.15	1.56
9	1.17	1.77	.48	1.29
10	1.08	1.84	.34	1.50
11	.77	1.49	.15	1.34
12	1.70	2.43	.95	1.48
13	1.38	2.44	.43	2.01
14	.83	1.23	.32	.91
15	.29	.52	.02	.50
16	1.43	2.17	.55	1.62

Highest Quartile, 100 cases, score range 22–40.
Lowest Quartile, 102 cases, score range 0–9.

ERRATA

Page 35, line 5, *for* 51.0 percent *read* 47.0 percent.
Page 132, line 25, *for* 51.0 percent *read* 47.0 percent.

tile has a score range of from 22 to 42. The lowest quartile, or the most pro-Jewish range in score from 0 to 9. In between the highest and lowest scores, the range is between 10 and 21, which may be considered the neutral range. Accordingly, 26.8 percent of the total 479 subjects were anti-Jewish, 51.0 percent were neutral, and 26.2 percent more or less pro-Jewish.

III. THE FIRST EXPERIMENT

THE BOOK OF PSALMS

THE Book of Psalms has a number of qualities that should make it an effective means for developing better understanding between Christians and Jews. The profound influence of these Hebrew religious poems on the Christian Church is well known. From the very beginning of Christianity, the Psalter has been the basis of Church liturgy and hymnology. That Christianity gave preferential status among the books of the Old Testament to the Psalms is indicated by the fact that when the New Testament was published apart from the Old Testament, the Book of Psalms was usually printed with it. Probably the Psalms are more frequently used by the Episcopal Church, the group with which this particular experiment deals, than by any other denomination. The Psalms are included in the "Common Prayerbook" and a psalm is read at every Episcopalian service. Because they are part of its religious belief and teaching and are also deeply interwoven in its daily ritual, the Psalms enjoy an honored position in the Episcopal Church and should possess high psychological valence for its adherents.

In the field of religious indoctrination, the authoritative prestige of the Book of Psalms is enhanced by its popularity. The Book appeals directly to the individual. It uncovers a wide range of human emotions: hate as well as love; vengefulness as well as forgiveness; the feeling of loneliness as well as of friendliness; doubt as well as faith. It describes not only the attributes of God but also the human need for security, companionship, and approval. The poets in this anthology are not only enthralled by the wonders of creation about which they sing praises, but they are also imbued with an all embracing sense of the worth and dignity of human beings whom they glorify. From these poetic elements and psychological insights is derived the verbal effect of this book of the Bible on religious attitudes.

For the particular purpose of this experiment, it should be recalled that the Psalms are also characterized by a universalistic spirit. Direct reference to ethical dealings with one's neighbor are numerous. It does not preach tolerance. Tolerance is negative, implies a degree of condescension and is at best passive. The Psalms rather exhort one to participate in a positive respect for and an active acceptance of the "stranger" who is frequently mentioned. "The stranger within thy gates" is to be treated as an equal, affirming the legal principle found in the Book of Exodus (Exodus 12: 49) "One law shall there be for the homeborn and for the stranger." In the Psalms such an attitude wins the approval of God and also achieves social and personal happiness on earth.

The stimulus material of the Psalms should be more than adequate for changing prejudice, if religious and moral preachment alone were effective in producing that change. In this particular situation, the Psalms were presented to the students by a Rabbi. Will anti-Jewish prejudice be reduced when this Jewish representative has the authorization of the Christian Church to teach religious material which emphasizes the very ideal of brotherhood? Will a knowledge of the Jewish origin of the Psalms be transferred into a measurable improvement in the attitudes of professing Christians to contemporary Jews? Will an appreciation of the spiritual contributions of the minority to the professed beliefs of the majority lead them to think more favorably of the minority?

THE INDIRECT GROUP METHOD

To repeat, these four factors are present in this experiment: the teaching of Biblical material with an emotional valence which emphasizes brotherhood as the ideal of true religion, the social familiarity of the Christian group with a Rabbi, the prestige of the Rabbi who enjoys the authorization of the Church, and the student's acknowledgement of Christianity's indebtedness to the Jewish people. It is hypothesized that these factors of the Indirect Group Method will modify anti-Jewish attitudes. Upon this hypothesis is based the approach to the first class of 49 communicants of the Episcopal Church of high school age. The mean age was 15.9. The group included 31 girls and 18 boys. In the initial test the mean score in the Jewish attitudes scale for this group was 15:10 with a standard deviation of 8.73 in a range of 0 to 42. Of the group of 49 students, 26.5 percent were anti-Jewish, 42.9 percent neutral, and 30.6 percent pro-Jewish. A digest of the stenographic report of the five fifty-minute sessions with these students conducted on five successive days will now be presented.

On the first day, the Rabbi introduced himself by referring to the invitation which the group's Church extended to him as evidence of Christianity's ideal of brotherly love. The avowed purpose of the novel situation which finds a Rabbi teaching Christians is to develop better understanding between Christian and Jew. While novel today, this was the only possible situation when Christianity first began, for then all Christians were Jews. Christianity's original dependence on Judaism was then illustrated by a description of the Jewishness of Jesus, the rabbinical training of Paul and the Jewish origin of the three major institutions of the Judaic-Christian tradition—the Bible, the Sabbath, and the democratic Synagogue or Church. The Rabbi explained the Jewish basis of the moral principles of the religion of Western civilization. "So very much of what a Christian believes, a Jew also believes, for modern Christian and modern Jew, both, have inherited their beliefs from the same source, from the Jews who wrote the Bible." Attention was then directed to the Psalms and the special importance of this Jewish book of religious poetry to Christianity and the Episcopal Church in particular. Reasons were advanced to account for the popularity of the Psalms. The Hebrew poetic form of the Psalms, known as "parallelism," was illustrated. In relating the history of the book, the Rabbi pointed out that this anthology included lyrical poems which were sung at the Jewish service in Solomon's Temple or by Jewish pilgrims on the road to Jerusalem. The majority of the Psalms date after the First Exile when many unnamed poets wrote them to inspire the individual Jew with courage and hope despite the hardships he was then suffering as a victim of tyrannical oppression. According to their spiritual message, God is universal and the wonders of nature testify to His greatness. Man should rejoice not only in this, but also in the fact that God insures the survival of those nations in which ethical relations between fellowmen are maintained. To triumph over defeatism and achieve this faith, to conquer hate and ill will in order that one might deal justly with one's neighbors, the individual should seek the support of God who is his Shepherd and Who expects such justice and love from His flock.

On the second day, the session opened with questions from students. They dealt with certain Jewish customs with which some of the students were familiar, like the wearing of the hat and prayer shawl in Synagogues. Upon request, the Rabbi illustrated the Hebrew language and chanted the Twenty-third Psalm according to the traditional mode. Spontaneous applause followed the singing. Stating that the class would study a number of Psalms which can aid the individual, the Rabbi asked the class to turn to Psalm 1 in their Bibles and discussed its definition of what comprises the "happy man." He preferred the translation "happy is the man" to the usual "blessed is the man" in order "to get out of your minds the idea that the Psalms refer only to how you feel in Church." That man is happy whose total personality is guided by the law of love in his acting and in his feeling as well as in his thinking. The Jewish ceremonial symbols, the phylacteries and the mezuza were described to illustrate how the religious Jew objectifies this idea. To the question "do many Jews change their religion" the Rabbi replied "I cannot give actual figures but I do not think many change their religion though they may change their names to evade discrimination against them when they are excluded from certain places or employment."

On the third day, the Rabbi further developed the idea of the undivided person in whom thought, emotion, and action are integrated. One who prays about brotherly love and acts contrariwise is at war with himself on the battleground of a guilty conscience. Psalm 15 illustrates that peace of mind comes to the integrated person whose test of religiosity is not what he prays, but what he does. The place referred to in the question in Psalm 15, "Who shall dwell in Thy tabernacle?" and the question in Psalm 24, "Who shall stand on God's holy hill?" is not a synagogue or church building, but any place on earth where a person establishes brotherly relations with his neighbor. By such action he makes that place "holy." This is dramatized by the vision of Isaiah (Isaiah 6) who concluded from this thought about the holiness of the whole earth that his own religious mission should not be the ritualistic function of his hereditary priesthood, but the teaching of peace on earth. Psalm 15, thus, defines the religious person as he "that worketh righteousness and speaketh the truth in his heart, that hath no slander upon his tongue nor doeth evil to his fellow, nor taketh up a reproach against his neighbor." The person who thinks himself superior and never shows respect for others as equals is not only irreligious, but also an unhappy person. "He hates other people," continued the Rabbi, "not because these people deserve to be hated, but because he needs to hate. He tries to escape what is wrong in himself by hating others. A person who hates is spiritually ill. The happiest time in a person's life is when he feels secure because he is loved, and others can love him only when he loves them." This is the kind of love God has for man which gives the believing man his sense of security in the world as portrayed in the well-known Twenty-third Psalm.

On the fourth day, the Rabbi described the three Jewish pilgrim festivals and gave Psalm 24 as an example of the antiphonal song which the pilgrims sang before the gates of the Temple. Here again one's worthiness of the privilege of entering the Temple is determined by one's actions toward one's neighbor. A student asked whether it was not impossible for an individual to change wrong attitudes even if he wanted to, since he is controlled by heredity or environment. In the discussion of nature versus nurture that followed, Psalm 27 was suggested as a realistic picture of some of the difficulties which the individual must overcome in nature—rivalry, war, and the possibility of being unloved and isolated. The Psalm indicates also that one can be demoralized by false accusations and by violent men who conspire against one. Yet it holds that despite competition, hate, and false propaganda the individual must face life with courage. On the other hand, Psalm 32 demonstrates how one can be made more unhappy by one's own inner world than by one's environment. Here the psalmist deals with the subject of a guilty conscience. In view of the modern findings of psychosomatic medicine, it is remarkable to note the way this Psalm describes the physical illness that frequently accompanies repressed feelings of guilt. Speaking in the language of modern psychotherapy, the psalmist claims that the only cure is to talk it out and relieve oneself of the burden of guilt. This observation of the Rabbi brought forth a discussion of the difference between confession and psychoanalysis. Psalm 35 was then referred to as illustrating how a person can be made unhappy by unjustified hostility. For no good reason at all, men may hate others and without cause issue vicious propaganda against them (Psalm 35:7, 11, 20). "They speak not peace, but they devise deceitful matters against them that are quiet in the land." The experience is even more painful when the victim has done good to the men who hate him. "They repay me evil for good."

On the final day, the Rabbi referred to Kant's dictum, "The starry heavens above and the moral law within," as being a good summary of the spiritual philosophy of the Psalms as a whole. This is most fully described in Psalm 19 where the universal presence of God is proven by the natural law He created and the equality of all men in God's eye is attested to by His sun which shines on all alike. The book's declaration that a nation survives only if it lives by moral law, is directly stated in Psalm 146. A nation survives not by her rulers but by her people who live according to God's way and God "executeth justice for the oppressed, giveth bread to the hungry, upholdeth the fatherless and the widow." The Psalm implies that the economic needs and social security of all must be provided for by the nation. Particular attention was directed to verse nine, "The Lord preserveth the stranger." Applied to America which includes Protestant, Catholic, Jewish, white and Negro citizens, these fellow Americans must become better acquainted with each other and the rights of all must be safeguarded, if America would continue to merit the blessings of God.

The following day the group took the post-test on the scale of attitudes toward Jews. The mean score was 15.61 with a standard deviation of 8.23 in a range of 1 to 33. The results indicate that 26.5 percent were anti-Jewish, 44.9 percent neutral, and 28.6 percent more or less pro-Jewish. Recalling that the post-test Form B shows a slight tendency to increase the score, we must conclude that the group showed *no significant improvement or worsening* in its attitude toward Jews after the course in the Psalms with the Rabbi. The comparison is indicated in Table 5.

TABLE 5

TEST AND RETEST SCORES OF INDIRECT METHOD

Connecticut Episcopal Group I (N49)

| | | | | PERCENTAGE | | |
	MEAN	S.D.	RANGE	*Anti*	*Neutral*	*Pro*
Initial Test Form A	15.10	8.73	0–42	26.5	42.9	30.6
Post-Test Form B	15.61	8.23	1–33	26.5	44.9	28.6

The score of the one extreme case was lowered from 42 to 30, but, nonetheless, remained in the anti-Jewish range. Twenty lowered their individual scores from 1 to 11 points; but 28 raised their scores from 1 to 14 points. Since the group as a whole showed no significant change, we conclude that despite favorable conditions the indirect method of teaching the democratic principles of religion and the specific Jewish contributions to these equalitarian ideals of Christianity did *not,* according to our measurement, change the attitude of Christians toward Jews.

In an item analysis the post-test shows slight increases in total scores on 12 items and slight decreases in total scores on only 3 items. On the other hand, there is a significant decrease in disagreement with item 14, "We are indebted to the Jews for their contribution to religion." On item 14, the chi square of the difference between the test and post-test is 10.74, significant at the one percent level (see Table 6).

TABLE 6

THE DISTRIBUTION OF THE NUMBER OF
RESPONSES ON ITEM 14 (N49)

	Agreement	Slight Agreement	Slight Disagreement	Disagreement
Initial Test	28	7	6	8
Post-Test	30	16	1	2

Thus, the learning and acceptance by the group of the Jewish origin of Christianity was increased but the group's anti-Jewish attitude did not decrease. It is equally significant to note here that there was a greater percentage of agreement than disagreement on item 14 among the most prejudiced highest quartile on the initial test. This indicates that the most prejudiced even at the outset agreed, despite their prejudice, that they were indebted to the Jews for their contribution to religion. The percentage of the most prejudiced who agreed with item 14 also increased after the course. Yet, despite this increased agreement on Jewish contributions to religion among the most prejudiced, the score of the total group on the attitude scale toward Jews did *not* decrease (see Table 7). Further statistical validation of the conclusion that the Indirect Group Method did not reduce the prejudice score of this Christian group in their attitudes toward the Jew will be presented when the results of the Indirect Group Method are compared with the results of the Direct Group Method.

TABLE 7

PERCENTAGE DISTRIBUTION OF RESPONSES ON ITEM 14 OF THE
MOST PREJUDICED ON THE SCALE—HIGHEST QUARTILE (NI3)

	Agreement	Slight Agreement	Slight Disagreement	Disagreement
Initial Test	38.4	23.1	15.4	23.1
Post-Test	38.4	53.8	——	7.8

THE DIRECT GROUP METHOD

The direct method was applied in the course on the Psalms presented by the same Rabbi to a class of 48 students, communicants of the Episcopal Church. They assembled for a one-week seminar in the same manner and from the same Connecticut communities as the first group of the previous week. The mean age was 15:6. The group included 32 girls and 16 boys. In the initial test the mean score for this group in the scale of attitudes toward Jews was 18.77 with a standard deviation of 8.21 in a range of 4 to 39. Of this group 41.6 percent were anti-Jewish, 43.8 percent were neutral, and 14.6 percent were more or less pro-Jewish.

The same kind of presentation of the Psalms was given to this second group as to the first group. It included the same history of the Jewish origin of Christianity, the same emphasis on the religious ideals of brotherly love, the same psychological interpretation of the same selection of Psalms, their Jewish background, their importance to the Christian Church, and their significance for the individual. Fewer details of this material were given to the second group to allow time for including direct reference to specific anti-Jewish attitudes. The Rabbi made direct application of the Psalms' insistence on equality for the "stranger" to the Christian's attitude toward Jews. He spoke of the ironic inconsistency of accepting the Psalms' religious ideal of brotherhood and rejecting the Jews who developed this ideal. He outlined the methods and baneful purposes of anti-Semitic organizations. He deliberately attempted to correct factual misinformation about Jews and he made particular effort to stimulate the members of the class to speak of their feelings about and their experiences with Jews. In other words, attitudes toward Jews, pro and con, were specifically brought out into the open, and analyzed as illustrative of the practical application of the authoritative religious message of the Psalms. The transfer was not left to chance. In the following digest of the stenographic report on the classroom discussion with this second group, only the additional direct stimulus material will be presented.

On the first day, after the same general introduction about all original Christians being Jews and about the novelty of studying the Psalms with a Jew, the Rabbi said: "Some of you may never have seen a Jew and have heard so many things about them and frequently against them that you might think they are quite horrible people. I remember a story told me by a Jew who some thirty years ago opened a little store in a rural district. For several days the local citizens passed by to take a hasty glance through the window, but not a single customer came in. For years in their single primitive church they had been hearing the word Jew used as a synonym for the devil. These innocent and sadly misinformed parishioners had never seen a Jew. They wanted to get a look at the horns of the new proprietor whose Jewishness frightened them. Jews do not have horns; they are just human beings exactly like other human beings. The only way to judge any person, Jew or Christian, is to know the person."

After describing the Jewish life of Jesus, the Rabbi asked how Christians can dislike Jews and practice discrimination against them and still profess Christianity which preaches the golden rule, especially since Jesus whom Christians love was also a Jew. The consistency of the Nazis was pointed out for they not only hated Jews but Christianity as well and set out to destroy Christianity because Jesus was a product of the Jews. After showing how the Psalms were originally written to inspire courage during a period of despair in Jewish history, the Rabbi suggested that the class could recapture the spirit of that period and the meaning of the Psalms if each member would try to imagine himself a Jew today (1946). The Nazi annihilation of six million Jews including the burning alive of Jewish infants who could have been guilty of nothing except being Jews was then described. As a group, the Jews suffered the heaviest casualty of the war, a total of one third were destroyed. Although only 10 or 11 million are now left in the whole world, some people still make the ridiculous accusation that the Jews control the other two billion. "If you were a Jew you would have reason to despair; if you were a Jewish boy or girl and could not get into a college or get a job just because you were Jewish, you would need something like the Psalms to keep up your hope."

On the second day, a student asked why Jews do not believe in Christ. The Rabbi replied that while the early Christian Jews believed Jesus was the Messiah, Jews today consider Jesus a great religious teacher produced by the Jewish people in the manner of the prophets of Israel. The Jews subscribe to the moral principles which Jesus taught, though they do not look upon him as Christ or Messiah. When the class was asked by the Rabbi to give an illustration of the Psalms' conviction that those nations survive which follow God's way, one student gave the Nazis as an example of a nation that fell and the Jews as a nation that survived. This was followed by questions about the different definitions of the Jews as a nation, a race, a people, or a religious group which the Rabbi explained. The Rabbi, then, asked what the class thought was the reason for the survival of the Jew despite long persecution. This is a verbatim report of what followed:

Student A: I think the Jews continue to live because they believe in God.
Student B: The Nazis were destroyed because they don't believe in God and burned Bibles.
Rabbi: Do you think it would be all right to believe in God and believe in the Bible and still burn people?
Student C: If you believe in God you can't be that cruel.
Student D: If you believe in God you aren't allowed to destroy people.
Rabbi: Even those who aren't just like you are?

Student D: You can't do that because that would be breaking a commandment—"Thou shalt not kill."

Rabbi: Well, can you destroy a person without killing him?

Student: What do you mean?

Rabbi: Can you make him feel so bad that he just wishes he were dead?
Could you do things to him to make him feel that life wasn't worth
living?

Student E: You mean hurt his reputation?

Rabbi: Well, something like that.

Student E: I know how a person can make you feel bad. When you
want to do something in life and someone comes along and says you
will never make it. Someone says you can't do it. They keep you from
your ambition.

Rabbi: You mean that's like destroying your faith in yourself. Somebody's trying to make you feel small, inferior. If that is what you mean
can, let us say, you do that to a Jew? I am bringing this up because we
were discussing destroying a person without killing him. The Nazis
killed Jews. Can you do something to Jews without killing them but
yet make them feel bad, as though they were nothing?

Student E: I guess when a Jew comes into a place and they say to him
you can't get in here because you are a Jew, he is made to feel small.

Student F: I don't know why the Jews have to feel that way. I think
they are the smartest and the richest.

Rabbi: What do you mean by that?

Student F: I come from a town and I have got some Jewish friends
there. They are always the smartest in school and the Jews are very
rich.

Rabbi: You say they are very rich?

Student F: Well, I don't say they are millionaires but three brothers own
a factory and one owns a store.

Rabbi: How many Jews live in your town?

Student F: Let me see, I guess there are about 12.

Rabbi: And you say they are all rich and smart? Would that lead you to
believe that all Jews are rich and smart?

Student G: There are plenty of Jews who aren't rich. I read about the
life of Irving Berlin and Eddie Cantor and they were from poor homes
down on the east side.

Rabbi: Yes, you are right about that. There are millions of Jews in New York who are poor and live in tenement districts and millions of Jews who live in Europe who are poor. Some in Poland are on the verge of starvation. Would it be safe to conclude from 12 Jews in your town that all Jews are rich? I don't think it is safe to make any sweeping statement about any group of people. That is what we call generalizing. If you know one or two or one-half dozen Jews can you say that all remaining 10,000,000 Jews are like that, whatever the few Jews you met might mean to you?

Student H: Well, how many Jews are there in New York City?

Student G: I think there are 7,000,000.

Rabbi: That's almost the total population of New York City. What about the Irish policemen? (Class laughter.) I don't think there are more than 2,500,000 Jews in New York City. There are actually only 5,000,000 Jews in the whole U.S. That's not a very large population out of 140,000,000.

Student I: I believe this talk about the Jews being rich is just a bunch of boloney and bunk.

Rabbi: As a matter of fact I don't think they are all smart either. We have a Jewish word which I think you ought to learn, called "schlemiel." I guess the best translation of that would be sort of a dope. There are all kinds of Jewish stories and jokes about Jewish schlemiels. I think you will find plenty of Jews who aren't smart at all. I don't say we are any dumber, but we are not any smarter either. You see it just isn't safe to make any sweeping statement about tens of thousands of people. In any group that numbers in the millions you will find no more smart ones and just as many dumb ones as you will find in your own group and in all groups.

On the third day after presenting Psalm 15, the Rabbi asked the class to give illustrations of this Psalm's admonition against slandering a neighbor. The following is a verbatim extract from the class discussion:

Student A: You know some people who go to Church and after the services talk about their neighbors.

Student B: Why, I've heard women talk in Church about other women.

Student C: There's a man who goes to Church on Sunday and swindles people on Monday.

Rabbi: Do you think it is irreligious to harm the good name and reputation of another person?

Student D: You were talking yesterday, Rabbi, about attitudes towards Jews. Isn't there a lot of gossip against the Jews?

Rabbi: Yes, there is. Could you give me an illustration?

Student D: Yes. I know a story about a Jewish family that moved into our town. They were refugees and the professor was teaching at Yale. When they rented a house on our street one woman kept talking about trying to keep them out because they wouldn't be good for the neighborhood. One day they did hang their bedclothes out of the window, in the morning, so this lady said: "See, I told you they'd ruin the neighborhood!"

Rabbi: What happened?

Student D: Well, after three years they moved away to another section of the city and everyone was sorry they left because they were such nice people.

Rabbi: I am glad to hear that. Do you mean the neighbors didn't mind the matter of the bedclothes?

Student D: Well, it seems that's what they do in Europe to air out bedclothes in the morning and when some friends told these Jews that we didn't do this in America, they stopped doing it.

Student E: I'm from the same town and I know that story. It's true. These Jewish people were disliked at first but they aren't now.

Rabbi: What do you think was the main reason they were disliked?

Student E: I think they were disliked just because they were Jews. It was just stupid or prejudice. The bedclothes was just an excuse. When we got to know them it was different. And I also think the lady who did all the talking just was the kind who gets pleasure out of stirring up trouble.

The Rabbi followed this student's observations with an analysis of how prejudice can be based on ignorance. He explained how prejudice can arise from a person's attempt to escape his own frustrations by taking it out on another person—"the scapegoat." Some try to blame the Jews when something goes wrong with themselves or when there is something they do not like but cannot change.

Student: I remember listening to the discussion of some people who didn't like the New Deal and Roosevelt. They said everything was wrong because he was influenced too much by Jews.

Rabbi: Yes, I've heard that false charge. Hitler used it in his propaganda. There are people who have been hurt by the war, or by the death of sons and others who are disappointed in the results of the war. Have you heard people relieve themselves of these feelings of sorrow or frustration, by linking them up with dislike for Jews?

Student A: I've heard people say that Jews made money in this war. While our boys were fighting, they stayed home and made money.

Rabbi: Yes, I've heard of that kind of talk. The Nazi propaganda machine tried to use it against our soldiers to demoralize them at the front. But what are the facts? The Army and Navy records show 550,000 Jewish men and women in the services and thousands of casualties. In only one Synagogue, the one I serve, there were several hundred in the service, many wounded and three killed.

The story of the hero pilot Colin Kelly and his Jewish bombardier, Meyer Levin, in sinking the Japanese battleship, *Haruna,* was told by the Rabbi. A student followed this with the remark: "Seems to me if a Jew is willing to be killed for America and defend us, he has the right to live on the same street with us." Another student made the same observation about some Armenians who had moved recently into his neighborhood. Referring to the statement in Psalm 15 that one must keep his oath to his neighbor, the Rabbi asked the class to recite the oath of allegiance to the flag as an example and applied the phrase "one nation indivisible with liberty and justice for all" to the need to resist propaganda that would divide groups against each other like Christians against Jews, and the obligation to assure a just opportunity for education and employment for all. A student then related this story: "There was a laundry in our town that had been abandoned for a couple of years and the people complained about there being no laundry service around. A Jewish fellow recently came to town and opened up that laundry and then the people began to talk about the ambitious Jews. Our rector told them off all right! Here was a fellow taking a chance to give them the service they need. They ought to be thankful instead of criticizing him." The period closed with a discussion of the Christian's responsibility for removing prejudice from his mind. Said one student: "I think its the job of the majority, after all, we have the prejudice."

On the fourth day at the request of a teacher of another course on "The Holy Communion," considerable time was devoted to a description of the Kiddush or the table service in the Jewish home on the Friday Sabbath evening and the Passover home meal service as some of these Jewish home symbols are carried over into the Communion service. The difference between the Jewish Sabbath and the Christian Sunday, the calendar relation between the Jewish Passover and the Christian Easter and the matter of Jewish dietary laws also came up for discussion. Then Psalm 146 with its message of economic security and equal treatment of the "stranger" as prerequisites for a nation's survival was applied to Christian-Jewish relationships. As an illustration, the Rabbi told the frequently quoted story about the Pacific Island natives who live off a certain breadfruit tree. When the tree's fruit is plentiful, they welcome strangers; when it yields only enough for the natives, they drive the strangers away; and when the tree fails to yield enough for the natives, the natives eat the strangers.

On the final day, these eight points were reiterated: (1) the Psalms which are part of the Christian belief were written by Jews and also are part of present-day Jewish belief; (2) the Psalms test belief in God by one's actions toward one's neighbor; (3) the American people will survive if they prove their professed belief in God by extending true equality to all; (4) from these convictions, we conclude that it is irreligious and un-Christian, unpatriotic, and un-American to deny to others rights we demand for ourselves; (5) the best way to break down prejudice is to get acquainted with other groups; (6) making the Jew a scapegoat for our mistakes or blaming him for our problems must be avoided; (7) discrimination can be reduced by improving the economic situation; and (8) prejudice can be lessened if we try to put ourselves in the other person's place.

"For example," said the Rabbi, "imagine that you are a Jewish girl with a good high school record who cannot get into college because you are Jewish. Imagine that you are a Jewish boy, a graduate engineer, and simply because you are a Jew you cannot get a job in a large corporation that you could serve well. Imagine that you are a Jewish soldier who lost an arm in the war. You are standing in a subway train in civilian clothes and you overhear a person saying, 'The Jews didn't do anything in the war.' How would you feel as you looked down at your empty sleeve? Imagine that you are a veteran trying to buy a house which the agent is ready to sell until he discovers that your name is Cohen. Imagine that you are a little Jewish lad coming home in tears to your mother, "The boys won't play with me because I'm a Jew." Here a girl student interrupted with the empathic remark "And imagine how that boy's mother was feeling, too!"

The Rabbi then asked the class to turn to Psalm 35 written by a Jew describing how he feels when he is a victim of unjustified hostility. Verses 19 and 20 introduced a discussion of specific anti-Semitic organizations and their efforts to gain political power in America by exploiting people's prejudices. The session closed, as in the first group, with a presentation of Psalms 19 and 146 and their appeal for brotherly relations in order to preserve a free nation and to secure God's blessings.

The students in both groups were required to keep notebooks which were handed in to the instructor. Further illustration of the difference between the Indirect Group and the Direct Group Method can be seen from the following examples of direct references to Jews which were found *only* in the notebooks of the second group taught by the Direct Group Method. "We must become better acquainted with the Jews who are strangers to us so we will not make statements that are not true." "Not all Jews are rich, there are many poor Jews in New York." "There were more than 500,000 American Jews in World War II." "The easiest thing in the world is to dislike a stranger; the reason a Rabbi was asked here was to break down strangeness." "Anti-Semitic organizations try to stimulate hatred against Jews. Beware of them." "Slandering a Jewish person is bad. They are just like us except for their religion."

"We should not make scapegoats out of American minorities. The more we find out about the Jewish religion, the more we understand the Jewish people." "All this regard to Jews is a lot of bull; if you can't live with them you should be nothing in our Lord's eyes." "Jews are human and friendly as are other people, and they have their ups and downs, happiness and sorrow." "There are only 10 million Jews in the world, why all this fuss and nonsense about their power?" "A Christian's attitude toward a Jew is a good test of whether he is a Christian or not."

On the post-test the mean score of the second group on the scale of attitudes toward Jews was 14.15 with a standard deviation of 9.40 in a range of 0 to 34. Of this group 20.8 percent were anti-Jewish, 43.8 percent were neutral, and 35.4 percent were more or less pro-Jewish. The group showed a significant improvement in its attitude toward Jews. A comparison of the test and post-test scores can be seen in Table 8.

TABLE 8

TEST AND POST-TEST SCORES OF DIRECT METHOD

Connecticut Episcopal Group II (N48)

	MEAN	S.D.	RANGE	PERCENTAGE Anti	Neutral	Pro
Test Form A	18.77	8.04	4–39	41.6	43.8	14.6
Post-Test Form B	14.15	9.40	0–34	20.8	43.8	35.4

The critical ratio of the significance of the difference between the scores of the test and the post-test is 4.47 (the correlation term is included in this calculation). The score of one extreme case was only lowered from 39 to 34; but another was lowered from 34 to 7. Eleven raised their individual scores from 1 to 13 points, but 37 lowered their individual scores from 1 to 27 points. There can be no doubt that, measured by our scale, the second method, which confronted the Christian group with its anti-Jewish attitude and the challenge of such attitudes to Christianity, to democracy, and to one's own personal stability, *did* change the attitude of Christians toward Jews.

The attack on anti-Jewish attitudes was made from many sides. It included corrective information, emotional persuasion, logical deduction, moral exhortation, and religious sanction. However, it was primarily distinguished by the class discussion which introduced the disapproval of anti-Jewish attitudes by one's own peers as well as by the authorized leader. Some student contributions bordered on the confessional and others approached a type of verbal release of aggression. Thus, the accounts of their experiences with Jews supplied a kind of psychological catharsis for anti-Jewish feeling within the group. The group was led to face openly the specific operation of anti-Jewish attitudes and the results which deny the professions of Christians and deter the progress of democracy. The focus was on group participation in discussions which were partly a catharsis for unexpressed hostility.

STATISTICAL COMPARISON OF THE TWO METHODS

A comparison of the results of the Indirect and Direct methods may be made by analyzing the scores of 27 cases in both groups matched for initial score. In this instance, the mean score for *both* groups on the initial test is 16.22. On the post-test for Group I, INDIRECT METHOD, the mean was increased to 16.37, the S.D. 7.49; on the post-test for Group II, taught by the DIRECT METHOD, the mean score was lowered to 10.93 and the standard deviation 7.83. The critical ratio of the difference in Group II is 3.12. The superior value of the second method for changing anti-Jewish attitudes is indicated in Table 9.

TABLE 9

TEST AND POST-TEST ON 27 CASES MATCHED FOR INITIAL SCORE

	GROUP I INDIRECT			GROUP II DIRECT		
	Mean	*S.D.*	*Range*	*Mean*	*S.D.*	*Range*
Initial Test	16.22	6.79	4–29	16.22	6.95	4–29
Post-Test	16.37	7.49	5–30	10.93	7.83	0–29

The single highest scores in both groups changed only one point suggesting that extreme anti-Jewish attitudes that border on the

TABLE 10

PERCENTAGE DISTRIBUTION OF THE SCORES OF 27 CASES
MATCHED FOR INITIAL SCORE

Connecticut Episcopal Groups I and II

	GROUP I INDIRECT			GROUP II DIRECT		
	Anti	*Neutral*	*Pro*	*Anti*	*Neutral*	*Pro*
Initial Test	25.9%	51.9%	22.2%	25.9%	51.9%	22.2%
Post-Test	29.6%	44.5%	25.9%	11.1%	44.5%	44.4%

anti-Semitic may not be appreciably affected by either method. In Group I, the "neutrals" shifted in both directions, increasing the "anti" and the "pro" group slightly; while in Group II there is a pronounced shift from the "anti" toward the "pro" group giving the latter a significant increase (see Table 10 and Figure 1).

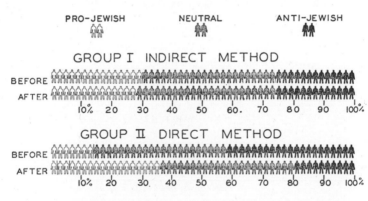

FIGURE I

DISTRIBUTION OF ATTITUDE SCORES AS CHANGED BY THE
INDIRECT AND DIRECT GROUP METHODS

Connecticut Episcopal

Additional statistical evidence of the greater effectiveness of the Direct Group Method over the Indirect Group Method in changing Christian attitude toward the Jew may be seen in a correlation of the individual scores and in an analysis of the variance of the scores. The correlation of the scores of the initial test and post-test of Group I, Indirect Method, is .83 indicating that the order of the individual scores remained more or less constant with very little change. This compares with the correlation of .85 of the *uninstructed* respondents on the scores of their initial test and post-test. However, the correlation of the scores of the initial test and post-test for Group II, Direct Method, is .68, indicating considerable change in the order of the individual scores (see Table 11).

TABLE 11

CORRELATION ANALYSIS CONNECTICUT EPISCOPAL GROUP

INITIAL TEST AND POST-TEST

Control Uninstructed W. Va. (N309)	.85
Group I Conn. Episcopal Indirect (N49)	.83
Group II Conn. Episcopal Direct (N48)	.68

TABLE 12

ANALYSIS OF VARIANCE OF POST-TESTS

Conn. Episcopal, Group I and II, Matched for Initial Scores (N27)

INITIAL TEST

	d.f.	Sum of Squares		F Ratio
Between	1	0	0	
Within	53	2546.34	4804	
Total	54	2546.34	4804	

POST-TEST

	d.f.	Sum of Squares		F Ratio
Between	1	400.16	400.16	6.69
Within	53	3170.15	59.81	
Total	54	3570.31		Significant at .05

An analysis of the variance of the scores of the two methods also supports the conclusion that the difference in the results of the Direct Method and the Indirect Method is not chance but a significant difference resulting from the different factors in the two methods. The F ratio is 6.69 significant at the 5 percent level (see Table 12).

The Indirect Group Method did *not* change the group's attitude toward the Jew. The Direct Group Method *did* reduce the prejudice of the group toward the Jew.

IV. THE SECOND EXPERIMENT

THE NAME "Old Testament" is now taken for granted, but historically it signifies an anti-Jewish attitude on the part of the classic Christian Church. In the development of the term "Old Testament" can be traced the background for a Christian's acceptance of the Bible and his rejection of the Jews who wrote it. Three major steps are involved in this ironic process. First, as a Jew, Jesus naturally depended on the Jewish Scriptures (on what Christians now call Old Testament). In the gospel biographies there are innumerable quotations from these Jewish sacred writings, the only literature Jesus knew. In these quotations, Jesus not only honored the Jewish writers of the Bible as the prophets of God's kingdom to come, but Jesus also considered the people of Israel as a whole to be the "chosen" messengers of this message. Even if we accept as genuine the much debated versions in the Synoptic Gospels where Jesus is quoted as having referred for the first and only time to "a new testament" (Matthew 26:28; Mark 14:24; and Luke 22:20) it can not be inferred by this statement that Jesus cancelled the "promises" of the old Mosaic covenant or that Jesus renounced Israel as the "chosen." In this first stage, then, the Old Testament and the Jews were given co-equal importance.

The second step occurred when Paul developed the thesis that the "promises" in Jewish Scripture foretell the coming of Christ. This served to enhance the religious value of these sacred books of the Jews to the new converts to Christianity. At the same time Paul was dissatisfied with the slow progress that was being made to convert Jews to Christ. Paul, therefore, turned to Gentiles and before them criticized his fellow Jews for their resistance to his particular interpretation of their Jewish Books. In Paul's epistle to the Corinthians the Jewish books of the Bible are referred to for the first time as "the old testament." "But their minds (meaning the non-Christian Jews) were blinded; for until this day remaineth the same veil untaken away in the reading of the old testament which veil is done away in Christ" (II Cor. 3:14).

The third step now logically followed. Soon Christians claimed that only a Christian could really understand and therefore interpret the sacred books of the Jews. Since these religious books were supposedly written for the sole purpose of foretelling the new covenant with Christ and since the Jews did not accept the Messiahship of Jesus, the Jews forfeited their own books.

The disinheritance of the Jews from their own sacred literature was finally accomplished in the writings of the Church Fathers (Parkes, 1934). St. Augustine declared: "the Old Testament is nothing but the New covered with a veil and the New Testament is nothing but the Old revealed." Addressed to Gentile Christians at a time when Jewish-Christians were no longer significant in the new religion is this warning from the epistle of Barnabas: "take heed to yourselves, and not be like some, adding largely to your sins, and saying: 'the covenant is both theirs (the Jews) and ours (the Christians).' " Accordingly, the Scriptures were no longer considered a part of the history of the Jewish people. In his *Ecclesiastical History,* Eusebius dates Christian history from the Genesis creation story and says it was "the Christ of God who appeared to Abraham, gave divine instruction to Isaac and held converse with Moses and the later prophets." [1] Christianity appropriated all that was good in the Old Testament; its heroes and leaders were incorporated into Christian hagiology. Moses became a Christian Saint (Parkes, 1934, p. 105). One of the Church Fathers, St. Irenaeus, the Greek Bishop of Lyons (c. 130–200) recognized the irony of the theological process by which Christians accepted, even glorified the

[1] Eusebius, *Ecclesiastical History,* I, IV; P.G., XX, p. 76.

writings of the Jews but at the same time vilified and renounced the Jewish people. With considerable sarcasm, Irenaeus wrote: "the Jews, had they been cognizant of our future existence and that we should use these proofs from the Scriptures which declare that all other nations will inherit eternal life, but that they who boast themselves as being of the house of Jacob are disinherited from the grace of God, would never have hesitated themselves to burn their Scriptures." [2]

Some heretical groups like the Gnostics, pushed anti-Jewish attitudes to a logical extreme. They rejected the Old Testament Books altogether and thus relieved themselves at one stroke of the difficult exegetical task of proving Christ from the Old Testament and of the embarrassment of the Jewish antecedents of Jesus (Grayzel, 1942). However, such heresy was not allowed to the majority of the Gentile Christians who continued the unhappy dilemma of loving the books of a people they were taught to dislike. This is the ideological conflict involved in the semantics of "The Old Testament."

Whenever a Christian uses the term "Old Testament" he unwittingly enters into a pattern of theological thought which is historically charged with an anti-Jewish attitude. However, when the Old Testament books are taught to Christians today it can be demonstrated with scientific historical facts that the Jews wrote these sacred books and that these books contain the actual history of the Jews. It also can be shown that there is a direct historical continuity between the Jews of the Bible and the Jews of the present who have kept alive the Hebrew language of the Bible. Furthermore, the Jews of today have maintained the Old Testament as the basic sacred authority of their present-day monotheistic beliefs in a living religion, Judaism. Such a scientific presentation includes an emphasis on the universalistic elements of the Old Testament which obliges Christian as well as Jew who together profess its authority to deal ethically with one another. Would this

[2] Irenaeus, *Cortia Haereses*, III, XXI; P.G., VII, p. 946.

approach to teaching the Old Testament change Christian attitudes toward Jews?

In a Leaders' Guide prepared (April, 1944) by the Board of Education of the Methodist Church of America and given to the Rabbi for teaching a course entitled "The Old Testament in the Life of Today" we read in the preface: "This is not merely a 'content' course; while the students should become familiar with the contents of the Old Testament, they should also gain insight into its value to us today, and understand and appreciate more fully the debt we owe to the Hebrew people whose religion forms the basis of our Christian religion today." We might assume that the phrase "the Hebrew people whose religion forms" refers to the Jews today, though this assumption would be clearer if the phrase read "the Jewish people whose religion forms," for the Jews of today are no longer called Hebrews.

In the days of Jesus the Hebrews were already spoken of as Jews, the people of Judea. As distinguished from the three Synoptics, the Gospel of John is characterized by a deliberate effort to associate the term "Jews" with those who opposed Jesus. The Gospel of John inferred that all the Jews were the opponents of Jesus. In John there is little indication that Jesus and his original followers were Jews.

Eusebius of Caesarea (c. 260–340), one of the most important church historians of the fourth century, based his whole treatment of the Jews on an artificial distinction between the words "Hebrew" and "Jew." Parkes says of Eusebius that "all the virtuous characters of the Old Testament, patriarchs, prophets and kings alike, he called Hebrews, and considered to be pre-incarnation Christians; all the evil characters he called Jews" (Parkes, 1948, p. 116).

Accordingly, the word "Jew" was used as a synonym for anti-Christian. This negative attitude is carried on whenever the people of the Bible are referred to only as Hebrews, thus disassociating them from Jews. It is as if the Hebrews ceased to exist with the canonization of the Bible and the Jews of today were totally unrelated to them. That this was not the intention of the Leaders' Guide is attested to by the fact that the Methodist Church invited a Rabbi, a representative of contemporary Jews, to teach the particular course on "The Old Testament in the Life of Today" to a group of young Methodist people.

The avowed purpose for this arrangement made by the Methodist Church was the development of better relations between Christian and Jew. By having the Rabbi teach the course, the Methodist Church hoped to bring home to the students the fact that the religious idealism of the Old Testament, an inextricable part of Christianity, is still being continued by the contemporary religious Jews, the descendants of the Hebrews. The Church also hoped that as a result of such a course, anti-Jewish attitudes within the Christian group might be reduced.

This hypothesis was the basis for inviting the Rabbi to teach three groups of Methodist students who elected to take the course entitled "The Old Testament in the Life of Today." In the Seminar prospectus it was announced that this course would be taught by a Rabbi. The Seminar was held at West Virginia Wesleyan College in the summer of 1947, but it was independent of the college administration. It was authorized and directed by the national offices of the Methodist Church and students attended from many communities throughout the state of West Virginia. The Seminars were held on three successive weeks for five days each. Each classroom session lasted one and one-half hours. Different groups registered for each week. In addition to the course taught by the Rabbi, the curriculum included "At Work for a Christian World," "Meaning of Church Membership," "Youth and Christian Worship," "Evangelism," "Missions," "Understanding Ourselves," "Stewardship of Life," and "Choosing a Vocation." The same courses were repeated each week. All faculty members were clergymen or professional workers of the Methodist Church. There were different faculty members for each week, but the same Rabbi taught the Old Testament course in all three Seminars.

THE INDIRECT GROUP METHOD

The total student body in the first week's Seminar numbered 163. All filled in the scale of attitudes toward Jews which was distributed by the Dean. The mean score was 17.22 with a standard deviation of 8.31. Of this number 146 took the post-test after one week and the mean score was 19.05 with a standard deviation of 9.32. Because some of the students failed to fill out the introductory information, the test and post-test for each individual could be matched for only 102 cases which comprise the control group for this first Methodist experiment. The mean score for this number in the initial test was 17.27 with a standard deviation of 9.32.

Twenty-one students of the group, 11 boys and 10 girls, elected to take the course with the Rabbi. The mean age was 15.9. Did the choice of the course by the group indicate that it had a more favorable attitude toward Jews than the general student body? The initial mean score of this group was 13.43 with a standard deviation of 6.95. The table of comparison between the class score and the general student body score would indicate a more favorable attitude toward the Jews on the part of the class.

TABLE 13

COMPARISON OF ASSEMBLY AND CLASS ON INITIAL SCORE

West Virginia Methodist Group I

	N	MEAN	S.D.	RANGE	PERCENTAGE *Anti*	*Neutral*	*Pro*
Assembly Control	102	17.27	8.13	1–42	29.4	53.9	16.7
Class Experiment	21	13.43	6.95	0–27	19.0	42.9	38.1

Each classroom session with the Methodist students was longer than each session with the Episcopalian group. A digest of the stenographic report of these sessions on five successive days follows. On the first day, the Rabbi stated that his presence before the class of Christians was testimony of the Methodist Church's good will toward Jews. As before the Episcopal group, the Rabbi described in detail the dependence of Christianity upon Judaism—the Jewish background of Jesus and Paul, the Jewish origins of the Bible, the Sabbath, the Synagogue or Church, and of monotheistic ethics. It was pointed out that the Old Testament is profoundly significant to Protestantism because it is Bible centered. Originally the Bible was written by Jews, about Jews, and for Jews only, and these Jews have never disappeared. They not only continue today a religion derived from the Old Testament, but they also have kept alive the Hebrew language in which Scripture was written. It should, therefore, not seem strange for a Jew to teach the course.

The Rabbi then explained that the Jews do not call sacred scripture Old Testament because they believe their present Judaism to be a continuing fulfillment of the religious philosophy contained in Scriptures which the Jews prefer to call the Torah. The three divisions of the Torah into the Five Books of Moses, the Prophets, and Other Writings were described. The Rabbi said that both the Old and New Testaments possess religious authority for Christians, but the Jews base their religious authority upon the Torah, that part which modern Christian and modern Jew in common hold sacred.

The historical evolution of the thirty-nine books of the Bible was presented. It was pointed out that because the Old Testament developed over a period of 1500 years, it contains different levels of cultural attainment. The lower levels derive from a more primitive period and do not possess the ethical values of the parts of the Bible which were created in succeeding periods of higher standards. The Old Testament must be read, therefore, with discrimination. The Jews who wrote "love thy neighbor as thyself" certainly lived at a time of greater spiritual advancement than those who lived under the earlier law of retaliation, under the "eye for an eye" standard of tribal days. The Rabbi demonstrated how the latter was completely abrogated by the Rabbis of the Talmud before the rise of Christianity.

A mimeographed chart prepared by the Rabbi in which each book is placed in its proper historical period was distributed to the class. Illustrations were given of the Hebrew language and of the prose and poetic style of the Old Testament. In selecting the portions of the Old Testament for the course, the Rabbi omitted the several passages which Christian theology claims predict Jesus as Christ. Discussion of these few controversial passages would only lead to theological debate, which obviously would have the "boomerang effect" of increasing antagonism.

On the second day the Rabbi outlined a naturalistic history of the Jews of Bible times. (For the course the class was required to read a very short text *The Story of the Old Testament* by Glenn McRae, selected by the Methodist Church). "The people of the book" were traced from the nomadic Patriarchal period to the Maccabean revolt against the Syrian Greeks. The influence of the desert environment on the psychology of these people resulting in the Biblical Jew's quest for freedom, his sense of hospitality, and his receptivity to spiritual contemplation, was analyzed. The free nomadic spirit was encouraged by the economic drive of the desert, namely, the search for water. The attraction of the "fertile crescent" fed by the waters Jordan, Tigris, and Euphrates stimulated recurrent invasions by the Semitic tribes of Arabia northward. The entry of the Hebrew tribes into Palestine, and their emancipation, unification, and legal organization under Moses and his successors was described.

The outstanding developments after the settlement in Palestine were the transformation from a nomadic to an agricultural life, the centralization of government under a monarch and the expansionism of Kings David and Solomon. The agricultural life introduced pagan ritual and fertility gods which conflicted with the former stricter desert religion and morality. The new political developments curtailed individual freedom and stimulated the concentration of wealth in a vested class which in turn brought about the growth of an indentured Jewish slave population. To correct these conditions of pagan ritual, political corruption, military expansionism, and economic injustice there arose the religious statesmen called prophets.

In their titanic struggle, the Jewish prophets developed a new revolutionary definition of God as the universal creator who judges all alike and guides history according to immutable laws of justice and love. They influenced the temporary "new deal" Deuteronomic Reformation of 621 B.C. However, despite their constant warnings the prophets were unable to effect durable enough changes to prevent civil war and the participation of the State in international wars. These wars ended in the destruction of both the northern and southern kingdoms of Israel and Judea. Palestine became the strategic military crossroads in the struggles of Egypt against Babylon and the first Jewish state did not survive the conflict. The Babylonian exile followed and later Nehemiah and his followers returned to rebuild Palestine under Persian tutelage. Palestine was later ruled by the Greeks after Alexander's conquest of the Persians. Eventually (165 B.C.) the second Jewish State was established after the successful Maccabean revolution against the Greeks.

During this whole period of 400 years from the Babylonian Exile to the Maccabean State two conflicting philosophies dominated Jewish thought: nationalism and universalism. Leaders like Ezekiel and Nehemiah (the Jewish Cromwell) sought to preserve the Puritanical uniqueness of the Jewish people and to make the Jews exclusive by ceremonial and legal identifications. On the other side, Jews, like the authors of Second Isaiah, Ruth, and Jonah, emphasized the universalistic character of God and held that Israel's mission was to teach the new moral religion to the world. Both attitudes stemmed from the belief that the Jews had a special function which they were "chosen" to perform in the world. When the Greeks appeared the two philosophies became thoroughly fused into a "religious-national consciousness." Religion and nationhood were united in a theocratic state. When part of that union, the political nation, was destroyed by the Romans, the religious identity of the group remained firmly intact and enabled Hebraism to survive the allurements of Hellenism.

The Rabbi concluded the introductory sessions by pointing out that because the Jewish people as an identifiable group with a profound religious loyalty survived, the Bible and Judaism, without which Christianity could never have been born, were preserved.

The last three sessions of the class dealt with specific selections from the Old Testament which have a bearing on contemporary problems. Because the material is so extensive, an artificial framework for a simplified presentation in three short sessions had to be devised. Three questions were posed. What could the world be like? Why is the world not like that? What can we do to make the world like that? To the first question answers were sought in the Torah (the Five Books of Moses), the first division of the Old Testament according to the Jewish religion; to the second question answers were found in the Niviim (the Prophets), the second Jewish division of the Old Testament; and for the third question the class was directed to the Kesuvim (OtherWritings), the third section according to the Jewish division of the Bible. In this division reference was made especially to the Psalms.

In the third session the Rabbi took up the first question by pointing out that the Old Testament immediately starts out with the Creation and Garden of Eden stories (Genesis 1 and 2) to describe what the world could be like. There we are presented with Judaism's hopeful affirmative view of life. This is dramatized in the recurring refrain of the Creation Story in which God says, "It is good," and in the exalted view of man, who is created in God's image. Life is good and man can choose the good in a fruitful world filled with an abundance for living. Although man has free will to choose the good, he suffers from his own envy and from the evil of his own making. Thus, man's violence destroys life's goodness as illustrated by the stories of Cain and Abel, of Noah, and of the Tower of Babel (Gen. 4, 6, 11).

To teach man how to choose the good life God inspires a man to instruct his fellow men in the way. This man is Abraham, the first Jew (Gen. 12). In the classic stories about his cooperativeness with his neighbor (Abraham's nephew Lot, Gen. 13), about his

hospitality toward the strangers (Gen. 18) and about his coura-
geous insistence on justice when he pleaded with God to save the
wicked cities Sodom and Gomorrah (Gen. 18), Abraham is given
as the example of how a righteous man can make his life "a blessing" to others. Even in men of great power the good conscience can
triumph, as exemplified in the lives of Jacob and Joseph who ulti-
mately conquer their inclination to deceit and boastfulness. At the
height of their successful careers these Jewish patriarchs display
honesty, humility, and forgiveness (Gen. 28, 32, 50).

Man must have an environment that is hopeful if he is to be
cooperative, kind, just, and forgiving. He needs freedom and he
can be free only if it is recognized that God holds each man's life
sacred. No other book in all history has inspired such belief in
liberty and a willingness to fight for it as the book of Exodus with
its account of Israel's liberation from Egyptian slavery. Its cry,
"Let my people go" (Exodus 5:1) and its parallel in the Book of
Leviticus "proclaim liberty throughout the land to all the inhabit-
ants thereof" (Leviticus 25:10) has resounded in every struggle
for freedom in history. It is celebrated in the Jewish festival of Passover which, the Rabbi said, Jesus was commemorating at the Last
Supper.

After freedom is won, said the Rabbi, the Torah illustrates that
law is necessary to protect the weak from the strong. Therefore,
after emancipation, Moses gave the Ten Commandments (Exodus
20) as a constitution and prescribed a system of justice (Exodus
18:20–21; Deut. 16:18–20) which proclaims equality to all under
law and specifically protects aliens and strangers from exploitation by the native born. To support law and orderly government,
man needs the influence of good religion to inspire him to become
a citizen of good will. Therefore, after giving the law, Moses established the sanctuary (Exodus 25) which is the basis of Synagogue
and Church.

However, political and religious institutions alone are no guaran-
tees for the good life. The individual himself must seek to live a
life of "holiness." He may be guided to this life by priests, taught

by ceremonies and holy days, and disciplined by dietary laws (The Book of Leviticus), but more important is it to achieve an attitude of neighborliness which is the personal act of holiness. This is the golden rule of Leviticus (Lev. 19:18), "Love Thy Neighbor As Thyself." Chapter 19 of Leviticus, known as the holiness code, describes each man's personal responsibility for making the world the place of peace and happiness it could be. This chapter describes the proper spiritual attitude toward the aged, enemies, strangers, and the poor. It is this chapter of the Old Testament which most influenced Jesus and which he quoted as the greatest commandment. Other passages in Leviticus (Lev. 25:39–43) and in Deuteronomy (Deut. 15:12–15) appeal for the liberation of men from slavery and extend kindness even to animals (Deut. 22:1–7).

In the Bible it states that to teach others what the world could be like Israel is elected. In performing this task Israel is prepared to face opposition such as the Book of Numbers describes in the Story of Balaam's Curse (Num. 22:12–16; 23:8–22; 24:9). Together with the story of the Pharaoh of Egypt (Exodus 1:8), this story of Balaam associates anti-Semitism not merely with opposition to Jews but with opposition to the religious teachings of the Jews. Despite persecution, the Jewish people accept the challenge of their destiny when they swear allegiance to God's covenant (Deut. 4). After hearing the final orations of Moses before he died, as recorded in the Book of Deuteronomy, the Jews pledged their loyalty to the task of making the world what it could be like. The dominant spirit of that agreement is love (Deut. 6:4–9) which Jesus later quoted as the second great commandment. This spirit of love is objectified in the Jewish ceremonials of the Mezuzzah and the Tefillin which the Rabbi described to the class. For living by the spirit of love man is rewarded with peace and plenty (Deut. 11:26; 28:1–6). Every man can choose to so live, for it is within his own inner power to do so (Deut. 30:19–20). Thus, said the Rabbi, the Torah, or Five Books of Moses, teaches us what the world could be like.

In the fourth session, the class considered the second question.

The Prophets declare that, because of man's ignorance and greed, the world is not the place of goodness and peace it could be. In his ignorance, man tries to placate God with ritual and sacrifice and clings to the notion of a tribal deity who will protect the members of his own group no matter how guilty they are. In his greed, man exploits the weak individual and wages war on other nations. He must learn from the external law of nature and the inner law of conscience that there are consequences to be paid for breaking the laws of morality. One can no more contravene the law of morality than he can break the law of gravitation. To ignore conscience and its demand that one must courageously insist on justice, peace, and brotherly relations for all regardless of color, creed, or country is to ignore God and doom society to destruction. The dramatic account of the rebellion of the Prophet Elijah against Ahab and Jezebel for their murder of Naboth and their theft of his vineyard was given as an illustration.

Because of the limitation of time only three of the shorter prophetic books of the Bible—Amos, Micah, and Malachi—were discussed by the Rabbi to highlight the prophets' views on what is wrong with the world. Amos accused the leisure class of crushing the poor to provide themselves with luxury (Amos 4:1). The corrupt members of this class attempt by name-calling to ostracize or silence all who in championing justice criticize the exploitation by the rich (Amos 5:7, 10, 11, 13). These persons are not only impervious to the sufferings of the many but they ignore their own self-interests since they are blind to the inevitable decline. Their prosperity is false because it is built on the impoverishment of the majority (Amos 5:21–24); only ethical dealings will save the situation (Amos 5:14–15).

Micah claimed that the whole social structure is corroded by acquisitiveness. When "every man hunts his brother with a net" (Micah 7:2) every element of social trust deteriorates. Even family life loses confidence and security in a purely competitive society (Micah 7:6). Yet, man can establish a golden age in which "swords shall be beaten into plough shares and spears into pruning hooks, nation shall not lift up sword against nation, neither shall they learn war anymore, and every man shall sit under his own vine and fig tree, and none shall make him afraid" (Micah 4:1–5). This peace will be achieved when man lives by true religion, which is not ritual but righteous conduct for "what doth the Lord require of thee, but to do justly, to love mercy, and to walk humbly with thy God" (Micah 6:6–8). Such conduct should be extended to all, for "Have we not all one father? Hath not one God created us? Why do we deal treacherously every man against his brother?" (Malachi 2:10).

In the final session, the Rabbi posed the third question: "What can we do to make the world like that?" According to the Bible, the world can become a place of plenty, freedom, peace, and good will for all if those who claim to be religious persons will practice what they pray and preach. From the Psalms we learn that it is the personal responsibility of every religious person, Christian as well as Jew, to make the world the kind of place it could be. Psalms 15 and 24 emphasize the conquest of hateful prejudices and the achievement of brotherly feelings toward all neighbors as the purpose of church membership and the proof of the individual's belief in God. The person who considers himself superior will neither respect others nor afford them equal consideration. Such an attitude of superiority is the denial of religion, for Christianity and Judaism require that the worth of every human being as a child of God be recognized. Psalm 146 declares that this cooperative attitude toward the other person, regardless of creed or color, is necessary if any nation is to survive. The different groups that make up America must learn to live with each other as fellow citizens, not as strangers. The equal rights of all to earn a decent livelihood must be maintained so that, by internal domestic example, America may lead mankind to an era of justice and understanding. (See Chapter III for fuller treatment of the Psalms.)

After the course was completed, the class took the post-test. The mean score was 14.00, the standard deviation was 7.33 in a range of 0–31. The comparison in Table 14 indicates no significant improvement *or* worsening in the attitude of the class toward Jews after the course in the Old Testament with the Rabbi.

TABLE 14

TEST AND RETEST SCORES OF INDIRECT METHOD

West Virginia Methodist Group I (N21)

	MEAN	S.D.	RANGE	Anti	Neutral	Pro
				PERCENTAGE		
Initial Test Form A	13.43	6.95	0–27	19.0	42.9	38.1
Post-Test Form B	14.00	7.33	0–31	19.0	57.2	23.8

The standard error of the difference is .30. The scores of two individuals remained unchanged, the scores of eight were lowered from 1 to 8 points and the scores of eleven were raised from 1 to 10 points.

The Indirect Group Method included teaching the Jewish origin of the Old Testament, the authoritative position occupied by these sacred books of the Jews in Christianity and the moral obligation which acceptance of the Biblical principle of brotherhood places on the Christian. We can conclude from the measurement of our scale that this Indirect Group Method did *not* appreciably change the attitude of this Christian group toward Jews. A more detailed analysis of this conclusion will appear when the Indirect Group Method is compared with the two other methods used with Methodist Groups II and III.

THE FOCUSED PRIVATE INTERVIEW METHOD

The following week a class of 25 out of the Second Seminar of 149 students selected the Rabbi's course in Old Testament. The mean score on the attitudes scale for the total Second Seminar group was 17.47 with a standard deviation of 7.84. Of this group 119 took the post-test in which the mean score was 18.64 with a standard deviation of 9.23. It was possible to match 115 of the tests and post-tests for the same individuals. The mean score on the initial test for this group was 17.03, standard deviation 8.37, and the mean score on the post-test 18.80, standard deviation 9.32. The initial mean score for the class was 16.36, standard deviation 9.18. The mean age was 16.5, 17 girls and 8 boys. A comparison of the class score with the total group score in the initial test is given in Table 15.

TABLE 15

COMPARISON OF ASSEMBLY AND CLASS ON INITIAL SCORE

West Virginia Methodist Group II

| | N | MEAN | S.D. | RANGE | PERCENTAGE | | |
					Anti	*Neutral*	*Pro*
Assembly Control	115	17.03	8.37	0–36	34.8	40.0	25.2
Class Experiment	25	16.36	9.18	1–36	24.0	48.0	28.0

The class shows an attitude slightly more favorable toward Jews than the general group shows, which may account for these students' selecting the course with the Rabbi.

The presentation of the Biblical material as given in the first Seminar was repeated. However, additional private interviews averaging thirty minutes each were arranged with each student during the week. The interviews were focused on encouraging the student to speak about his personal relations with and his attitudes toward Jews. The Rabbi began each private conference with the following:

"I was very pleased when I received the invitation from your national office in Tennessee to lead your class. It is a great honor to have your Methodist leaders place so much confidence in me and I want you to know that I am deeply grateful. I suppose they wanted you to have the opportunity of meeting a Jew and of studying the Old Testament with a Rabbi, since, as we have been studying in class, the Old Testament was written by Jews and the Bible is today believed in by both Jews and Christians alike. It occurred to me that while the class is being given a Jewish point of view, I should learn about the Christian point of view, since understanding each other is a two-way proposition. I suggested these private interviews because we could not take the class time for each of you to present the Christian viewpoint. You've expressed your willingness to spend these few minutes with me. I find that I will not be able to remember what each member of the class says unless I take a few notes. If this is all right with you, I'll do so."

Examples of a number of cases will be presented here.

The case of P——, who is a girl, 17 years old, in the 12th grade. Her father is a minister in a large city. Her initial score was 1, the most favorable toward Jews in the group. Her score on the post-test after the interview and the completion of the course was 0.

Rabbi: Do you have any Jewish contacts?

P: My best friend is a Jewish girl. I go to school with her, we like each other.

R: Do you know her family?

P: Yes, they belong to an Orthodox Church, but they don't follow all the rules like Kosher meals. Her father is a traveling salesman.

R: What are your feelings toward them?

P: I like them fine and I like her family and her friends. We get along fine.

R: Do your good relations with this Jewish family account for your attitude toward other Jews?

P: I never thought about it consciously, but I think it has a lot to do with it.

R: Would you say your attitude was different before you met this Jewish family?

P: I don't think so. I was pretty young and a child doesn't think much about these things. But I never heard anything in my home against another race or religion. They just don't talk about it—about anything bad and that helps form one's opinions.

R: You have heard other people talk about Jews?

P: O, yes, I'm afraid so. They talk about Jewish people owning stores, but I've read a lot about race prejudice—it's a habit. I am interested in statistics, so I know they're not true because they seem to think the Jews control the clothing business and people tell jokes and talk about them not very nicely.

R: What is their basis for talking about them?

P: Well, I said before many people don't know them. I have another girl friend. I don't agree with her views. She's always ready to talk about the Jews. And I think her family must have a lot to do with it. The family is sort of bad about talking about other people, especially against Negroes.

R: Do you think people talk about Jews because Jews are that way, or because these people have a need to talk about Jews?

P: I feel they have a need to do it. A sort of an inferiority complex makes them take it out on somebody. They build up in the years ideas from their grandparents and parents. Therefore they have bad ideas about the Jewish people. This makes the Jewish people's children feel peculiar. The more sensitive ones among them feel that the Gentile student feels that way about them, and therefore the Jewish children stick together. They sort of get in a rut there. In our school they're not much of a problem. It's when you get out by yourself in groups and if the subject comes up, then they don't talk as nicely about Jews as before. In our school the Jewish kids are very popular in X——. Probably it is different in different sections of the country.

R: Do you recommend any way of solving or treating this problem?

P: Well, I don't know. By the time the student gets in high school or college, unless they're fair-minded, it's much too late to change them. I've tried it on different people, but they don't pay attention. Parents I suppose have most to do with it. They influence the very young. I am most fortunate because my parents are liberal. When they talk they have a different attitude, and of course I've read a lot about how these ideas get started and that's the way I feel about it.

R: What started you reading on the subject?

P: I can't remember where my interest started, but I read books, lately Tannenbaum's *MUST MEN HATE?*. It's a very good book and I got a hold of it by just seeing it in the Public Library and I took it out.

R: What kind of a plan could the Christian Church adopt to influence Christians about this matter?

P: Well, it would have to be done through the proper understanding of the problem. If you could get somebody you trust and they like you, you could influence them so much more than if you just tell them what you think. It's the personality they like and that counts. I've thought about it, but I have no plan that would change these sort of opinions. Of course, the Christian Church can do it as much as possible—in the Sunday School especially where the children are younger. Here you probably could work most with children and then the ministers and people like that should show older people the difference, but I don't know how well that would work.

R: Could there be some experiences in the Sunday School which would serve to make prejudice against Jews?

P: No, I don't believe so. There's nothing around the Church, but there are plenty of workers in the Church who have prejudices. Our young people's counsellor told us she couldn't stand colored people. She was brought up that way and realized it was wrong, but she couldn't keep herself from feeling that way. That's the way with most people. They think they are so right when they hate and if you get them to believe maybe they're wrong, yet they still feel that it is not right that they should be influenced.

R: Do you think that it is mostly the person that counts in causing prejudice?

P: Yes, like I said. People judge a group by the individual. If you know the people and you like them, you have a good opinion of the whole people.

R: Do you think that the kind of person teaching this class would make any difference in the results?

P: Yes, although not entirely. I think a lot of it depends on the kind of person, even if people don't realize it. I think they all like the class, they talk about it and they seem to be enjoying it.

R: Do you think we could do more to add to the effectiveness of this class?

P: I think you're doing okay. I can't think of anything specific myself. Of course, you teach about the Old Testament and Jewish history and that is not teaching race relations. I would like to hear statistics about the problems. How many people do this or that.

R: Do you feel that I ought to deal more directly with this problem?

P: Some people might not like it. It's sort of hard to think about other people and face the facts.

R: Do you think that if I would say something about the great Jews like Einstein, or Heifetz it would do any good?

P: I don't know. If talking about that sort of thing is good in this class it might seem like boasting and dragging in of something. It is hard to try to get people to form new opinions. This is a class in

Old Testament. Of course, it might be the thing to do. You have to have a lot of experience and know how people would react.

R: Do you think there can be some counter-measure that might be effective?

P: I don't know. If you already have the right attitude it makes you feel good to hear this sort of thing but if you're set in your ways, what you may say about great Jews may be fine and very good, but the others would still say I don't want the Jews around here. I don't know what to do with that kind of person.

R: Do you think that it is a real problem, threatening to the Jews of America?

P: I don't think it is now. It's not that bad. I think perhaps the problem of the colored people is much worse. There are people who are more friendly toward the Jews than they used to be. I feel that way. It'll get better rather than worse from now on. I can't tell, of course, but the Jewish children now are so much more a part of the rest of the country. They get in more contact with Christians.

R: What do you think about inter-marrying with the Jews?

P: I don't know. It's all right personally, but my girl friend is going to go to a college like Ohio State because her parents say that there are no Jewish boys in other colleges and they want her to meet a Jewish boy to marry. I see that. It makes it much harder when Protestants and Jews get married and maybe that's one reason why the Jewish people keep themselves separate. Probably one of the persons marrying will have to change religions. I suppose one could keep his or her religion, but then there's the children.

R: Would you recommend inter-marriage?

P: I would if the two could make it work and if one is willing to change the religion for the other, but otherwise it would cause more trouble than anything else. That's the trouble. You don't know just what would be the case and marriage is difficult and then you'll also have religion to cope with.

R: You seem to have a mature insight into these problems. Did you receive this background from your family?

P: My father is a minister. Of course as a minister he stands for brotherhood although I've heard him say things I don't like and I tell him so, but he's pretty good considering the average. My mother is a quiet woman. She was brought up in a small town and has a liberal point of view. She had no contact before with Jews and she is not one of those people who do not like others because they don't know them. What she doesn't know she will not say she doesn't like and she never said anything bad against people. I have a little brother of eleven and he has the same attitude. He's probably too young to think about it. He used to play with a colored child, and this might have had something to do with it and he goes to school with Jewish children. Whenever he stays anything about it, however, I try to show him what I think.

R: What would you like to do in life?

P: I'd like to be an artist, but I don't think I've got enough talent and maybe I'm a bit lazy. I'm really not sure what I want to do yet, maybe social work. I've been thinking about that more lately, especially along the lines of our conversation.

The case of I——, who is a boy 15 years old, in the 11th grade. His father (deceased) was a manager of a Gas Company in a small town. His initial score of 36 was the least favorable toward Jews in the class. His score on the post-test after the interview and the course of studies was 12.

I: I live in A—— Md., 45 miles from B——, W.Va., a town of 2,600.

Rabbi: Are there any Jews there?

I: Oh yes. There's a pretty nice family, the X——, who operate a chain clothing store, called the Half Price Store.

R: Do you have any contact with them?

I: We own the largest hardware store and they own the largest clothing store. Our grandfather gave the store over to his sons and one of my cousins who is 29 is a partner in our store and he goes with one of the older boys of the Jewish family, and I go with them sometimes.

R: Is this the first Jewish family you've met?

I: No, my father was once manager of a gas company in W——, and we lived beside 4 Jewish families.

R: Boys your own age?

I: Yes. One family was no good. They were too self-centered to suit me. They even thought they were too good for the other Jewish families. When you asked them to play they would say they had other things to do. One Jewish boy named G—— was fine, but the other boy didn't go with us. He was an introvert.

R: You've heard Christians talk about Jews?

I: Yes. They say they push too hard and too fast, trying to buy up everything and trying to get a monopoly and not leave anything for the Christians.

R: You feel that's true?

I: It's true for some Jewish families. One of them in W—— was trying to monopolize the clothing trade and he cut down on his prices to drive the others out and then he would jack up the prices later.

R: What about the other Jewish family?

I: No. He was in the clothing business too, but his prices were the same as the others. He belonged to a clothing syndicate and the other Jew didn't.

R: Isn't it possible to have a specific experience with one Jew and then apply it to all Jews?

I: I think it is. You think of the Negro being unkempt and then you think they're all that way. You can make the same statement about Jews or Catholics, which wouldn't be true. But there are Jews I like better than white people or Christians. You see one Jew and then you may set him for a standard for the rest and that's not right.

R: How can we handle this problem?

I: Do you mean how we can combat it? Promote understanding. In A—— there are some who are against Jews, but there are good and bad and we don't resent them. They're some who conduct good business like the whites and good Christians.

R: Do you know of any Jews who are poor?

I: I'm sure there must be some who are poor. It's wrong to make a general statement that they are all rich. You can't say one thing about a whole race.

R: Do you think that the attitude of the Christians towards Jews is an important problem?

I: I don't think so. You don't have race riots like against the Japs on the West Coast. It's a problem to be dealt with, but there's no impending disaster. It can be settled sensibly.

R: What would you recommend as sensible?

I: Take a poll of what the white Christians have against the Jewish race and of what the Jewish people have against the white race and both sides give half way each and teach understanding. No shooting —that's what Hitler did.

R: Do you feel Jews have something against Christians and Christians against Jews?

I: Yes, it's an equal proposition.

R: Have you heard about Jews keeping Christians out of hotels and colleges?

I: No, but Jewish business firms will not take Christians. But there are more Christian firms that won't take Jews.

R: Do you know of any Jewish boys who have trouble getting into college?

I: Yes, and it's no good. Some Jews do harm to the country, but that's overridden by what good Jews do. I think that Jews are fairly good for the country and should have an equal chance. If 10 boys apply to a school and one or more of them were Jews and were better students, they should get in and not the Christians, but I know of a college that didn't fill up its classes and still won't let Jews in.

R: Do you think that if people are given correct information such as the fact that 500,000 Jews were in the armed forces and many were killed, that there are Jews who do other things beside operate stores, and that there are more poor Jews than rich Jews, do you think this information would help change prejudice against the Jews?

I: I don't think it would. The whites would say it's just a story and they don't want these things thrust in their faces and they would say that the Jews just had it written for themselves and it would do more harm.

R: If information that is true is not effective, what do you think would be effective?

I: I'd do two things to get the unbiased truth. First I would do what you are doing—interviewing—and second I'd write a book that the white people would buy of their own accord. If they bought it of their own accord and read it, it would not be like propaganda.

R: This talking together you think helps?

I: Your talk changed my views. You know that we took an attitude test at the beginning of the week. It was given out by the dean. My answers would have been different if I would have talked with you first. In that short a time you can change if you have an understanding talk. My oldest cousin is a Jew hater and I am influenced by him and something like this straightens you out. I like my cousin, but he is against everything, Communists, yellows, blacks, and Jews. He is 24.

R: How did he get that way?

I: He was shot up in the war. Oh, he's mentally all right, but he says the Jew boys in his company were in the band. They never got shot up and two of his buddies were killed by a land mine while he got a fractured skull.

R: In my small congregation there were 250 boys in the services, three of them were killed, one of them by a land mine.

I: In our church there were about 180. Three of them got killed the same day, one on a ship and the other in the Bulge.

R: Well, it seems that both Christians and Jews were killed. I want you to know that I appreciate very much your taking the time to talk with me.

I: If there is anything else, just ask me. I shall be glad to come up to your office again any time.

The case of J——, a boy, 15 years old, in the 10th grade. He lives in a large city. His father operates a crane in a railroad shop. His initial score was 35, decidedly unfavorable toward Jews. The post-test score of 19 showed considerable change.

Rabbi: There are a number of Jews in your city. Do you have any contacts with them?

J: None, just buying in their stores.

R: Do you live near Jews?

J: No, the Jews have their own residential district.

R: They sort of keep together?

J: Well, I don't know so much about that. As far as I know they stick together. My only contacts are in their stores.

R: Is it possible that Jews are not permitted to live in your section?

J: That may be.

R: Is there any reason for doing that?

J: No, none I can see.

R: There are hotels that won't accept Jews.

J: I didn't know that. Our swimming pool may be restricted for I never saw a Jew there. I wouldn't know, of course, if the person were a Jew or not but in the stores I meet Jews. Nine of 10 stores are Jewish.

R: Do you hear about restricting Jews in colleges?

J: I think it is unfair from my point of view, just as unfair to keep the colored from voting. After all we are made up of every nation, just the same as the Irish or the Italians ought to get a start in America.

R: Have you heard Christians talk about Jews?

J: Yes, only in reference to their stores. They own the nicest places.

R: You hear remarks about that?

J: The remarks are always something against the Jews—mostly, that they are chiselers.

R: How do you mean?

J: Well, Jews always have higher prices and at the next door store owned by a white American the prices are lower.

R: You have actually had such an experience?

J: Yes, in this case the Christian American can't get the goods and the Jew can. How the Jews get them I don't know, but they always have it and prices are higher. Whereas if the American gets them in you can get it cheaper.

R: You think the Jew has a secret way of getting the goods?

J: No.

R: Is the identical item cheaper in what you call "the white American" store than in the Jewish store?

J: Yes, for example, a store owned by a white American had a double breasted suit I liked for $38, but not just the color I wanted. I wanted a tan but it was light blue. The Jewish store had the exact same suit in tan and wanted $50. I wound up with the blue.

R: Do more people want tan than blue in that style suit—gabardine?

J: Oh yes. My light blue suit isn't exactly what I wanted.

R: Isn't it possible that because more people want tan than blue, the tan is higher in price?

J: Come to think about it, we did study something in social studies class about demand makes the price. But, still I bet when the American store gets the tan suit, it will be cheaper.

R: Yes, that's quite possible. When the tan suit is not in such great demand and is easier to get, the price should come down. Though, I should think if the Jew wants to stay in business he would have to compete and the price of his tan suit should also come down.

J: You mean the price of the suit has nothing to do with whether the store is Jewish or white American?

R: Do you think this could be tested? Did the Jewish store have a light blue suit and was it higher?

J: No, they didn't, only the tan and I sure was disappointed that I had to buy the blue because of the difference in the price.

R: By the way, I notice you call one store Jewish and the other, white American.

J: I guess you should say Christian and Jewish stores. Jews are white, aren't they?

R: Yes, and of course they are also Americans. Do you think it would help relations between Christians and Jews if some of these facts about Jews could be straightened out?

J: Yes, if we get to know them better, we might change. You can dislike any person but when you see the person you can change. Now, I don't have prejudice but I've heard so much and you get to believe it.

R: Do you think if people got clearer the facts about Jews, such as that there are many Jews who do not own stores, that many are workers, or farmers, that Jews are good Americans for 500,000 of them were in the army and thousands died for our country in the war—do you think these facts would help change prejudices against Jews?

J: Yes, it might.

R: Do you think it is an important problem for Christians and Jews to understand each other better?

J: Oh, yes.

R: I want to thank you for helping me to see the Christian point of view.

It is interesting to note that because of both boys' prejudices against Jews, they do not consider the Jew "white." Both are from the South where color is deeply involved in prejudice against outgroups.

The mean score on the post-test taken by the class after the completion of the course and interviews was 10.84, standard deviation

6.03, in a range of 0–23. The group showed a *significant improvement* in its attitude toward Jews. The test and post-test scores compare as follows:

TABLE 16

TEST AND POST-TEST SCORES OF FOCUSED INTERVIEW METHOD

West Virginia Methodist Group II (N25)

	MEAN	S.D.	RANGE	PERCENTAGE *Anti*	*Neutral*	*Pro*
Initial Test Form A	16.36	9.18	1–36	24.0	48.0	28.0
Post-Test Form B	10.84	6.03	0–23	4.0	56.0	40.0

The scores of three students whose attitudes were the most unfavorable toward Jews were lowered from 36 to 12, 35 to 19, and 32 to 16 respectively. Sixteen others lowered their individual scores from 1 to 15 points while only 6 raised their scores from 1 to 9 points. The critical ratio of the significance of the difference between the scores of the test and post-test is 3.52 (correlation term included).

This method gave the student the opportunity to express, in private interviews, hostility against Jews; it gave the teacher the opportunity to direct the Christian student's thinking about the un-Christian and un-American character of specific anti-Jewish prejudices; and it allowed the student to focus his own personal experiences with Jews toward achievement of a better insight into those relations. Measured by our scale, this Focused Private Interview *did* change the attitude of this Christian group toward Jews.

THE DIRECT GROUP METHOD

The following week a class of 25 out of the Third Seminar of 116 students selected the Rabbi's course in Old Testament. The mean score on the attitudes scale for the total group was 15.40, standard deviation 8.94. Ninety-six took the post-test in which the mean score was 17.40, standard deviation 8.91. Ninety-two of the initial tests and post-tests could be matched for the same individuals. For this number the mean score achieved on the initial test was 15.08, standard deviation 8.31, and on the post-test 16.66, standard deviation 8.67. The initial score for the class was 11.84, standard deviation 6.31. The mean age was 16.8; there were 22 girls and 3 boys. A comparison of the class score with the total group score in the initial test is given in Table 17.

TABLE 17

COMPARISON OF ASSEMBLY AND CLASS ON INITIAL SCORE

West Virginia Methodist Group III

	N	MEAN	S.D.	RANGE	PERCENTAGE		
					Anti	*Neutral*	*Pro*
Assembly Control	92	15.08	8.31	1–36	23.9	44.6	31.5
Class Experiment	25	11.84	6.31	1–29	4.0	56.0	40.0

The same presentation of the Old Testament given in the first Seminar was repeated. As in the case of Connecticut Episcopalian Group II, fewer details were presented in order to allow time for including in class discussion direct reference to specific anti-Jewish attitudes. Members were encouraged to relate experiences with Jews pro and con. The origin of prejudices and the effect of these prejudices upon the emotional life of the prejudiced as well as upon the victim were analyzed. An ethical attitude toward neighbors which is given religious sanction by the Old Testament was carried over into a direct application of Christian attitudes toward the contemporary Jewish descendants of the characters in the Old Testament. When factual misinformation about Jews came up, it was corrected; when anti-Jewish experiences were related the class was guided to think of the un-Christian and un-American aspects of these experiences.

From the stenographic report of the class discussion the following is presented as an example of this direct method during one session.

When Abraham was described as the first Jew, attention was

drawn to Chapter 12 of the Book of Genesis where the first Jew is commissioned by God to bring the blessings of religion to mankind that the world may be saved from destruction. According to the Old Testament, those nations which accept the Jew, who comes to them at first as a stranger, will survive, "And I will bless them that bless thee"; but those who reject the Jew will fall, "And him that curseth thee will I curse." Egypt, Babylon, Rome, Spain, Germany were given as illustrations of the disappearance or the decline of nations which persecuted the Jews. History confirms the Bible's warning that attitude toward the Jewish minority or any minority is the spiritual barometer that measures the difference between barbarism and civilization. "In thee (the Jew), shall all the families of the earth be blessed."

The members of the class were then asked whether they found in their own experiences with Jews the kind of a blessing the Old Testament describes. Four in the class of 25 said that to their knowledge the Rabbi was the first Jew they had ever seen. One girl said that she lived beside two Jewish neighbors. One, a Jewish doctor she liked very much, but the other family "took flowers from her garden." Others spoke of Jewish school companions. One said the Jews were not friendly, while another declared them to be too friendly. One student said he assisted a Jewish schoolmate who did not reciprocate his help. A girl followed this boy and suggested that it was unfair to generalize about all Jews from one experience. The boy admitted that he did generalize and that it was wrong to do so. Another student declared that more favorable contacts with Jews would help to eliminate generalizations. An example was offered by a student who lives in a community where there is a single Jew who is a shoemaker. The shoemaker is considered strange because he will not accept every pair of shoes for repair and this is attributed to the fact that he is a Jew. He is also unmarried. From this, said another student, the Christians there might draw the ridiculous conclusion that all Jews are bachelors and eccentric. If Jews are different, another said, it is because "of the conditions under which they are forced to live; their lives reflect the treatment they receive" and "people who have no close relations with Jews cause all the trouble." One of the four who never met a Jew before said she held no opinions but her parents did not approve of Jewish neighbors. Another said, "Everybody has a little of the Jew in him since Adam was the first man and he was a Jew." The Rabbi corrected this novel view of anthropology.

"If many anti-Jewish attitudes do not come from actual experience," asked the Rabbi, "what are the causes of these attitudes?" One answered that Jews do the same things that Christians do, for human nature is the same, but Christians take more notice of the Jews and are more critical. At this point a girl related an event in her high school in an exclusive community in Ohio. A single Jewish family lived there before restrictions were imposed, and thus one Jewish boy attended the school. A son of a member of the Board of Education played a childish prank which went unpunished but when the Jewish boy did the very same thing, a great deal was made of it in order to compel the Jewish family to leave the community. The Rabbi asked whether this was fair play according to good Americanism or good Christianity. "It is because too many Christians think Jews are foreigners and not Americans that these unfair situations arise," answered a student. Discussion of this false assumption brought up restrictions in hotels and colleges and the question of intermarriages, and one student introduced the novel *Gentleman's Agreement,* as an illustration of these problems and of the unfair treatment of the Jew. When the Rabbi suggested that prejudice against Jews had a bad effect on Christians even as it was hard on Jews, one student declared, "the Jews have the most actual hardships." Another added humorously, "but the Christians have the hardest work trying to think up ways to keep the Jew out of things."

The Rabbi, thereupon, described the hard work involved and the careful organization which the Nazis set up to liquidate six million Jews and stated that this planned job of killing innocent people required the employment of thousands of Germans. "Could these persons be called Christians even if many went to churches before the rise of Hitler?" he inquired. One student said they were forced to do this killing; another said they had no Christian training; a third said "the Christianity they had didn't stick or they would have refused to do such work." "But," said the Rabbi, "at the Nuremburg Trials some of these executioners said their work was right because Jews are evil and even subhuman." One student answered: "They were affected by Hitler's propaganda which is just stupid; a Jew is a human being and if you are a Christian you cannot be prejudiced against them, and you should not be influenced by forces of prejudice around you."

"Then how can we explain the strange fact that Christians who know Jesus was a Jew dislike Jews nonetheless?" asked the Rabbi. Answers included unfavorable personal experience with Jews and prejudiced environment in the community and in the home. As effective methods for reducing prejudice, students suggested more contacts with Jews, education, broadmindedness, and an understanding of how we get prejudiced beliefs. The Rabbi suggested that the kind of talking out of their feelings that the class was doing would help to clarify their relations with Jews and overcome misunderstandings. He compared it to letting all the air out of a tire before patching a puncture (Gordon Allport's analogy). As long as persons begin with some indefinite dislike or a vague fear of Jews, any failing that a Jew may have in common with other human beings is magnified. But one student stated that the fact that all Jews are rich is a definite grievance against them. The number and status of poor Jews in the world was described by the Rabbi and it was necessary to correct one student who thought Andrew Mellon was a Jew.

It was agreed that though in many small towns the only Jewish contact a Christian may have is with a middle-class storekeeper, the ratio of poor Jews to rich Jews is probably the same as the ratio of poor Christians to rich Christians. "Even if this information were correct, it would not change prejudice against rich Jews," said one student. The economic basis of prejudice was analyzed and the discussion was carried over to the next day when envy was emphasized as a cause of Jewish prejudice. This led to an analysis of prejudice as an escape for a feeling of inferiority and as an alibi for frustration. A Jew may be prejudiced against a Christian because that Jew is treated as an inferior by the Christian; and a Christian may be prejudiced against a Jew because that Christian unknowingly feels inferior to successful Jews. "Love thy neighbor as thyself," said a student, "would cure all this." The Rabbi agreed that we fail to love our neighbor frequently because we do not love ourselves properly. Each person, Jew or Christian, must have more faith in himself and then he will have more confidence in the other fellow. "Certainly," concluded the Rabbi, "Abraham in the Old Testament offers such exemplary religious conduct to Christian and Jew alike in his treatment of the three strangers."

Similar class discussions took place each day about such contemporary topics as the loyal Americanism of Jews versus the false charge of Jewish Communism, the forced segregation versus the voluntary clannishness of Jews, the Jewish-Arab relations in Palestine, the equality of opportunity for Jews in education and employment, and the application of Christian principles of brotherhood toward Jews. Various passages and stories in the Old Testament led to these topics. The class listened to some members express hostile attitudes and to others who presented favorable attitudes. The class was directed to analyze prejudice and to think of the un-American and un-Christian and detrimental results of anti-Jewish prejudices.

On the post-test the mean score of this class was 7.72, standard deviation 6.86 in a range of 0–31. The group showed a *significant improvement* in its attitude toward Jews. A comparison of the initial test and post-test scores can be seen in Table 18. The score of the student whose attitude was the most unfavorable toward Jews was raised by two points, from 29 to 31; however, the next highest score was lowered from 21 to 2. Twenty-one lowered their individual scores from 1 to 13 points while only 4 raised their scores from 2 to 8 points. The critical ratio of the significance of the difference between the scores of the initial test and post-test is 2.95 (the correlation term is included in this calculation).

TABLE 18

TEST AND POST-TEST SCORES OF DIRECT METHOD

West Virginia Methodist Group III (N25)

| | MEAN | S.D. | RANGE | PERCENTAGE | | |
				Anti	*Neutral*	*Pro*
Initial Test Form A	11.84	6.31	1–29	4.0	56.0	40.0
Post-Test Form B	7.72	6.86	0–31	4.0	24.0	72.0

This method allowed the Christian students as a group to consider specifically their own anti-Jewish attitudes and to give verbal expression to hostility. It directed the group to think of the implication of these attitudes to democracy, to one's own emotional stability, and to Christianity itself. This Direct Group Method, measured by our scale, *did* change the attitude of Christians toward Jews.

STATISTICAL ANALYSIS OF THE THREE METHODS

We can make a further comparison of the results of the three methods, Indirect, Focused Interview, and Direct, by analyzing the scores of 16 cases in each of the three groups matched for initial score. Each group was compared with a control group selected from each of the three assemblies matched for initial score with the experimental group. In this instance, the mean score of all six groups was 13.31. On the post-test for Experimental Group I, Indirect Method, the mean score was 13.25, standard deviation 5.65; for Experimental Group II, Focused Interview, the mean was 9.88, standard deviation 5.40; for Experimental Group III, Direct Method, the mean was 7.75, standard deviation 7.16 (see Tables 19 and 20, and Figure II).

TABLE 19

TEST AND POST-TEST 16 CASES MATCHED FOR SCORE AND DISTRIBUTION
OF 0-1-2-3 RESPONSES ON INITIAL TEST

Group I, Indirect

	INITIAL TEST			POST-TEST		
	Mean	*S.D.*	*Range*	*Mean*	*S.D.*	*Range*
Control I	13.31	6.33	3–27	13.45	7.17	0–24
Experimental I	13.31	6.27	3–27	13.25	5.65	5–23

Group II, Interview

Control II	13.31	6.51	1–27	15.68	10.20	1–31
Experimental II	13.31	6.63	1–27	9.88	5.40	0–20

Group III, Direct

Control III	13.31	6.24	3–29	15.87	8.28	6–31
Experimental III	13.31	6.36	3–29	7.75	7.16	2–31

TABLE 20

PERCENTAGE DISTRIBUTION OF 16 CASES
MATCHED FOR INITIAL SCORE, EXPERIMENTAL GROUPS

	Anti	*Neutral*	*Pro*
Group I, Indirect			
Initial Test	12.5	56.25	31.25
Post-Test	12.5	62.5	25.0
Group II, Interview			
Initial Test	12.5	56.25	31.25
Post-Test	——	50.00	50.00
Group III, Direct			
Initial Test	6.25	62.5	31.25
Post-Test	6.25	37.5	56.25

Final evidence of the superiority of the interview and direct
methods over the indirect method for effecting changes in attitude
toward the Jew can be seen in a correlation analysis and in an analysis of the variance of the scores. The correlation of the initial test

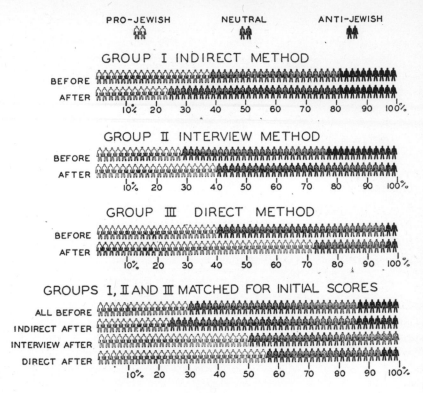

FIGURE II

DISTRIBUTION OF ATTITUDE SCORES AS CHANGED BY THE
INDIRECT, INTERVIEW, AND DIRECT GROUP METHODS

West Virginia Methodist

and post-test of Group I, Indirect Method, is .81, indicating that the order of the individual scores remained constant with very little change. This compares with the correlation of .85 for 309 respondents (uninstructed) on initial and post-test scores. However, the correlation of the initial test and post-test for Group II, Interview Method, and for Group III, Direct Method is .55, indicating considerable change in the order of the individual scores (see Table 21).

TABLE 21

CORRELATION ANALYSIS, WEST VIRGINIA METHODIST
EXPERIMENTAL GROUPS

Initial Test and Post-Test

Control, Uninstructed (N309)	.85
Group I, Indirect (N21)	.81
Group II, Interview (N25)	.55
Group III, Direct (N25)	.55

An analysis of the variance of the three methods supports the conclusion that the difference in the results of the Private Interview and Direct Group Methods as compared to the Indirect Group Method is not chance but a significant difference resulting from the different factors in these methods. The F ratio is 3.08, significant at the 1 percent level (see Table 22).

TABLE 22

ANALYSIS OF VARIANCE TABLE

*West Virginia Methodist Groups I, II, and III
Matched for Initial Score (16)*

INITIAL TEST	d.f.	Sum of Square	F Ratio
Among	2	——	0
Error	45	——	
Total	47	——	

POST-TEST	d.f.	Sum of Square	F Ratio
Among	2	246.166	3.08
Error	45	1797.7500	
Total	47	2043.9167	Significant at .01

The statistical analysis confirms the fact that a significant change in attitude is achieved by the Private Interview and Direct Group Methods. In the groups matched for initial mean scores, the mean of Group III, Direct Method, changed from 13.31 to 7.82, while the mean of Group II, Interview Method, changed to 9.50. We observe that the Direct Group Method which involved the class in direct discussion of anti-Jewish attitudes and allowed for a guided catharsis of hostility and reorientation of values brought about the greatest change in attitude.

The students were asked eight months later in an Information Questionnaire (see Chapter VI) whether their opinions were or were not changed by the course with the Rabbi. When the students themselves consciously declared whether their opinions were changed, those who were subject to the Direct Group and Focused Private Interview Methods showed a higher percentage who answer affirmatively than those who were subjected to the Indirect Group Method. While 57.5 percent of 59 respondents subject to the Indirect Group Method said the course did *not* change their opinion, 54.7 percent of 75 respondents subject to the Direct Group and Focused Private Interview Methods declared the course *did* change their opinion. The difference in each group between those who answered "yes" and those who answered "no" to the question "Did the Rabbi's course change any opinions you may have had about Jews?" is statistically significant. For the group taught by the Indirect Method, the chi square of the difference between the "yes" and the "no" is 9.6 significant at the 1 percent level; for the group taught by the Direct and Interview Methods the chi square is 6.6 significant at the 4 percent level. This verbal reaction of the students themselves to the different methods is further corroboration of the superiority of the Direct Group and Private Interview Methods over the Indirect Group Method.

V. THE STABILITY OF THE CHANGE IN ATTITUDE TOWARD THE JEW

WE HAVE demonstrated that the Direct Group and Focused Private Interview Methods change Christian attitudes toward the Jew and that the Indirect Group Method produces no change in attitude. We shall now investigate whether these changes in attitude are temporary or stable. Eight months after the Episcopal and Methodist experiments, each subject received the measuring scale by mail for recheck. The scale combined Forms A and B, stating eight items in the declarative form and eight in the interrogative form and is referred to here as the stability test. The scale was mailed from the office of Dr. Goodwin Watson, Professor of Education, Teachers College, Columbia University. It was attached to a letter signed by Dr. Watson which said in part:

"This letter is being sent to all who attended the Young Peoples' Conference this past summer. You will recall that the Dean, Reverend—— asked you then to join in an experiment which is being conducted by a group of psychologists at Columbia University Teachers College. This experiment is part of an effort to find out how different groups in America feel about each other.

"In connection with this experiment you will remember that you filled out a questionnaire on your attitude toward the Jews. Your cooperation and straightforward answers were greatly appreciated.

"In order to complete the study it is necessary to get your attitude now. For this purpose a questionnaire is enclosed. Will you take a few minutes of your time to fill it out. Do not put your name on it. Please be as straightforward as you can. Do not try to recall how you answered before; just check how you feel now. Please do not consult others, for the experiment will be successful *only* if the answers given are your own."

Returns were received from 45 of the 49 students in Group I, Connecticut Episcopalian; 38 of the 48 students in Group II, Connecticut Episcopalian; 15 of the 21 students in Group I, West Virginia Methodist; 22 of the 25 students in Group II, West Virginia Methodist; and 17 of the 25 students in Group III, West Virginia Methodist. Of the total 168 students 81 percent returned this third stability attitude scale. The scale was returned by 86 percent of the 70 students taught by the Indirect Group Method, by 75 percent of the 73 students taught by the Direct Group Method, and by 88 percent of the 25 students who were given private focused interviews. There was no significant relation between those who did not return the questionnaire (19 percent) and the degree of prejudice of this group. By prearranged markings on the stamped return envelopes and personal information on the tests, it was possible to match the stability tests individually with the previous initial tests and post-tests.

An examination of Table 23 which gives a complete summary of the tests in all experimental groups reveals the striking consistency between the mean scores of all groups on the third test and their mean scores on the second test. Whatever is the change or lack of change in attitude score after the courses with the Rabbi, that attitude score is maintained eight months later after the students had returned to their separate communities.

TABLE 23

SUMMARY OF TEST SCORES OF ALL EXPERIMENTAL GROUPS

Connecticut Episcopal

	GROUP I, INDIRECT (N49)		GROUP II, DIRECT (N48)	
	Mean	S.D.	Mean	S.D.
Initial Test	15.10	8.73	18.77	8.21
Post-Test	15.61	8.23	14.15	9.40
Stability Test	(N45)16.40	9.71	(N38)13.37	8.12

GROUPS I AND II MATCHED (N27)

	I		II	
	Mean	S.D.	Mean	S.D.
Initial Test	16.22	6.79	16.22	6.95
Post-Test	16.37	7.49	10.93	7.83
Stability Test	(N23)16.96	9.18	(N23)11.70	7.37

West Virginia Methodist

	GROUP I, INDIRECT (N21)		GROUP II, INTERVIEW (N25)		GROUP III, DIRECT (N25)	
	Mean	S.D.	Mean	S.D.	Mean	S.D.
Initial Test	13.43	6.95	16.36	9.18	11.84	6.31
Post-Test	14.00	7.33	10.84	6.03	7.72	6.86
Stability Test	(N15)12.94	5.64	(N22)9.77	6.74	(N17)8.12	5.40

GROUPS I, II, AND III MATCHED (N16)

	I		II		III	
	Mean	S.D.	Mean	S.D.	Mean	S.D.
Initial Test	13.31	6.27	13.31	6.63	13.31	6.36
Post-Test	13.25	5.65	9.88	5.40	7.75	7.16
Stability Test	(N13)14.08	4.71	(N13)9.23	5.02	(N12)7.83	4.88

A correlation analysis of all three tests reveals the effect that the different teaching methods had on the order of the individual scores, and shows whether that order maintained itself eight months later in the stability test (Table 24).

TABLE 24

CORRELATION ANALYSIS OF ALL EXPERIMENTAL GROUPS

	Initial Test and Post-Test	Post-Test and Stability Test	Initial Test and Stability Test
Group I Conn. Episcopal Indirect Method	.83	.75	.75
Group I W.Va. Methodist Indirect Method	.81	.82	.89
Group II Conn. Episcopal Direct Method	.68	.82	.71
Group III W.Va. Methodist Direct Method	.55	.75	.61
Group II W.Va. Methodist Focused Interview	.55	.57	.55

Table 24 gives a correlation analysis in all experimental groups between initial test and post-test, post-test and stability test, and initial test and stability test. In Group I, Connecticut Episcopal and Group I, West Virginia Methodist taught by the Indirect Group Method, these correlations are practically the same. The relative positions of the individuals remained fixed between initial test and post-test, post-test and stability test, and initial test and stability test. It will be recalled that the correlation between the initial test and post-test of 309 in an uninstructed control group is .85. For the Connecticut experimental group subject to the Indirect Method the correlation between the initial test and post-test is .83; between the post-test and stability test .75 and between the stability test and initial test also .75. For the Methodist Group Indirect Method, these correlations are even closer to the correlation between the initial and post-tests, which is .81. Between the post-test and stability test, the correlation is .82 and between the initial test and stability test it is .89. Thus, the order in the attitude score of the individual students, subject to the Indirect Group Method of teaching remains fixed throughout, proving again no change in attitude score. The attitude toward the Jews with which all the classes in the Indirect Group Method started the courses is unchanged and remains the same eight months later.

In the groups subject to the Direct Group Method of teaching we have previously noted (Tables 11 and 21) the considerable change in the order of the individual scores. In the Connecticut Direct Method Group the correlation between initial and post-test is .68; and in the West Virginia Direct Method Group it is .55. Furthermore, that change in order of the individual scores remained stable eight months later. This is indicated by the fact that the correlations within the post-test and stability test are high for both the Connecticut and West Virginia Direct Method Groups. For the Connecticut Group the r is .82 and for the Methodist group .75. That the change remained stable once it did change is indicated by the fact that the difference between correlation of the stability test and the initial test (Connecticut r .71; West Virginia r .61) and the correlation of the *post-test* and initial test (Connecticut r .68, West Virginia r .55) is only .03 for the Connecticut Direct Method Group and only .06 for the West Virginia Direct Method Group. There can be no doubt that a change in attitude toward the Jew was effected by the Direct Group Method and that this change remained stable eight months later.

Of special interest is the correlation analysis of the individual scores of subjects taught by the Focused Private Interview Method. The correlation of the post-test with the initial test shows a considerable change in the order of the individual scores, the r is .55. The r of the stability test and the initial test is also .55. In other words, the subjects in the Focused Private Interview Method changed their attitude toward the Jew and this change in attitude is maintained eight months later. However, the order of the individual scores in the stability test when correlated with the order of the individual scores in the post-test does not produce a correlation coefficient as high as does the correlation of these two tests in the Direct Group Method (.82 and .75). The correlation coefficient of the stability test and post-test of the Focused Private Interview Method is .57. In the Direct Group Method when the change in order took place after the course, it settled down and remained fairly fixed eight months later. However, in the Focused Private Interview Method after the change in the order of the individual scores took place, the scores of these individuals continued to change, shifting positions eight months later.

It will be recalled that in the Direct Group Method the entire class participated in a discussion which was specifically focused on attitudes toward the Jew. The change in attitude in this situation had reference to a group experience, where one's own peers expressed disapproval of anti-Jewish attitudes and where there was the involvement of the group to which each member belonged and from which he derived his new social values. In other words, the change in attitude was reinforced by the knowledge of how other people in one's group feel. The Focused Private Interview Method, on the other hand, produced a change in attitude as the result of a face to face discussion with one Rabbi. He was the primary factor in the experience which changed the attitude. Such a single reference did not make the individuals as secure in their new attitude as did their own group reference. Therefore, while the change in total attitude brought about by the Group Direct Method remained stable eight months later as far as each individual in the group was concerned, the change in the total attitude brought about by the Private Focused Interview technique did not remain stable eight months later as far as each individual was concerned.

Finally, an analysis of the variance of the scores on the stability tests of the groups matched for Initial Score (see Tables 12 and 22 for analysis of variance on post-tests) validates the conclusion that the change in attitude scores of the total groups remained significantly stable eight months later (see Tables 25 and 26.)

TABLE 25

ANALYSIS OF VARIANCE OF STABILITY TESTS

Connecticut Episcopal Group I (N24) and II (N23) Matched for Initial Scores

	d.f.	Sum of Squares		F Ratio
Between	1	325.28	325.28	4.47
Within	45	3273.83	72.75	
Total	46	3599.11		Significant at .05

TABLE 26

ANALYSIS OF VARIANCE OF STABILITY TESTS

West Virginia Methodist, Group I (N15), Group II (N22), Group III (N17) Matched for Initial Scores

	d.f.	Sum of Squares	F Ratio
Among	2	272.4972	5.28
Error	35	902.8975	
Total	37	11.75.3947	Significant at .01

The difference in the attitude scores between the groups subject to the Indirect Group Method and groups subject to the Direct Group and Focused Private Interview Methods remains statistically significant eight months later in the Stability Test. We conclude that the changes in attitude affected by the Direct Group and Focused Private Interview Methods were retained eight months later.

Because the group taught by the Direct Group Method reduced the mean of its attitude score more than did the group taught by the Focused Private Interview; because the change produced by the Direct Group Method remained more stable throughout than did the change produced by the Focused Private Interview, we conclude that the *Direct Group Method is superior to the Focused Private Interview in modifying Christian attitudes toward the Jew.*

VI. THE RELATION OF VERBAL

BEHAVIOR TO CHANGE

IN ATTITUDE

I T IS appropriate to inquire whether a change in attitude toward the Jew as indicated by the attitude scale is something
more than just an overt verbal change. Is the change in attitude transferred to new behavior toward the Jew? For example,
do subjects who reveal pro-Jewish attitudes on the scale present
favorable views toward the Jews when they participate in their
own group discussions about Jews? Do subjects who indicate pro-
Jewish attitudes defend the Jew when they witness anti-Jewish incidents or remarks? Item 10 in the scale is: "People who are not Jewish should try to answer those who say things against Jews." Do
subjects who agree with this opinion, act on this attitude? At the
suggestion of the late Dr. Ruth Benedict, an effort was made in this
study to examine this relation between attitude and behavior on
these scale items.

To the 97 students in the two Episcopal experimental groups
and to the 71 students in the three Methodist experimental groups,
a separate Information Sheet was distributed by mail from the
office of Dr. Watson eight months after the courses of study with
the Rabbi (see Appendix A, Form C). Question 3 in that form
asked: "Since studying the Psalms (or the Old Testament) with
the Rabbi eight months have passed. During this time, has there

been any discussion or conversation about Jews in your Church group? If answer is Yes, state here what it was about. What did you say?" Question 4 asked: "During the past eight months has there been any incident or remark concerning Jews which you witnessed or heard? If answer is Yes (omitting names of persons) describe the incident or remark here. What did you think of the incident or remark? If you did or said anything in the situation, what did you do or say?"

VERBAL BEHAVIOR IN GROUP DISCUSSIONS ABOUT JEWS

On Question 3 of the Information Sheet, of 137 respondents, 53 or 38.2 percent reported participation in their own communities in group discussions about Jews, during the eight months that had elapsed since the course with the Rabbi. Most of these discussions took place in a church youth group in which the respondent was a member. A few took place in other social groupings.

Some of the respondents' examples of these discussions will be presented here. The selections are from respondents who were subjects of the Indirect Group, of the Private Interview, and of the Direct Group teaching method. Each of the three scoring categories in the attitude scale, the most prejudiced, the neutral and the least prejudiced are also represented. These reports are from the Information Sheets which were returned unsigned. However, by certain pre-arranged markings on the return envelopes, it was possible to match each report with the individual's attitudes tests.

Examples of respondents subject to the Indirect Group teaching method follow.

Case A illustrates the verbal behavior of one who did not change her attitude, despite the fact that she increased her awareness of Jewish contributions to Christianity. This case is a girl of 15, from a small town, Connecticut Episcopalian, I.Q. 125 (all I.Q.'s were determined by the Otis test). Her father is a Colonel in the United States Army. She records having no Jewish friends. Her score is consistently anti-Jewish; 26 on the initial test, 29 on the post-test, and 38 on the stability test. Indeed, she became increasingly anti-Jewish, as she learned more about Jewish contributions to Christianity. She writes in answer to the question on group discussions about Jews: "We simply talked about the Psalms and the beauty of them and how the Jews are a very poetic people. A few words of prejudice came in about why not send them back to where they came from so they can write some more poetry. I said I felt sorry for the poor Arabs who would have to have their country overrun with them."

Case B, girl, 16, from a large city, I.Q. 111, Connecticut Episcopalian. Her father is an electrical engineer. She records having "10 and many more" Jewish friends but was consistently anti-Jewish in all her scores, 29, 26, and 24. To the question on discussions about Jews she writes: "If you let very many of them into a Club or organization of any sort they feel they should lead it and be the head of it. They try to take over all positions and order you around. I was inclined to agree as I have seen it happen many times. We have an English Club and they have taken it over."

Case C, boy, 16, small town, I.Q. 93, Connecticut Episcopalian. His score remained consistently neutral 15, 15, and 14. He writes that in his group: "The President suggested to go to a Synagogue to attend a service and have the Jewish come to our meeting. I agreed to it but others said no."

In the least prejudiced category in the groups taught by the Indirect Group Method the following are some reports of the respondents on group discussions about Jews.

Case D, girl, 16, city, I.Q. 103, father an inspector, Connecticut Episcopalian. Her scores were 8, 6, and 7. She writes: "There have been discussions as to how difficult it is for Jews to enter the college of their choice because of racial prejudice. I said: 'Jews should be allowed fully as much freedom as anyone else; that is the only way the U.S. can call itself free.' "

Case E, girl, 17, I.Q. 139, small town, Connecticut Episcopalian. Her father is a milk dealer. She records having 10 Jewish friends and considerable experience with Jews. Her score was consistently pro-Jewish, 0, 1, and 1. She writes: "Someone said that Jews are very grasping, always work only for the betterment of the living conditions of their own race, and are entirely too numerous in our government as well as our city. I said that Jews have as much right to be in politics and business as anyone else, that they are to be congratulated for working for the betterment of anything and that they are no more grasping or selfish than members of any other race."

Case F, girl, 16, small town, Connecticut Episcopalian. Her father is a textile technologist. Her score was pro-Jewish on all three tests, 6, 4, and 9. She writes: "We spoke about any Jews we know in school and named them. We then tried to see if they did anything differently. The Jews I know in school fit right in, they are very active, even more so than others."

Case G, girl, 17, I.Q. 118, West Virginia Methodist, small town. Her father is a coal miner. Her score remained the most pro-Jewish throughout, 0 on all three tests. She writes: "I told the group about what I learned from the Rabbi at Assembly. It helped all of us understand Jews better. I explained the fact that the Jews believed in the Old Testament but not the New. In spite of that fact they were good people and I liked them."

Case H, girl, 16, I.Q. 98, West Virginia Methodist. Her father is a fireman. Her scores were consistently pro-Jewish 4, 7, 9. She writes: "The question was asked in our group: Do you think Jews have too much control in the community? I said no. They have as much right to state their feelings as well as we do. This is their country. We must always remember Jesus was a Jew."

From the groups taught by the Direct Group and Private Interview Methods which changed attitudes toward the Jew come these reports about group discussions about Jews.

Case I, the most prejudiced with the initial score of 36, a boy, 15, I.Q. 129, 11th grade, father deceased, small town, West Virginia Methodist (Interview Method; see interview page 78). His score of 36 changed on the post-test to 12 and on the stability test it was 7. He writes: "The Palestine question. I said they ought to have it."

Case J, a boy, 15, 10th grade, large city, father a crane operator, West Virginia Methodist. (Interview Method; see interview page 81). His initial anti-Jewish score of 35 changed to 19 on the post-test but went back to 31 on the stability test. He writes: "About the Jew merchants and what awful high prices they charge; and the Arab-Jewish business in Palestine. I said all Jews are not alike and I mentioned the Rabbi and what a nice person he was; and I don't think the Jews should try to take over Palestine." This case confirms the general statistical findings about the instability of attitude changes effected by an interview with the Rabbi. The favorable impression created by a single member of a minority is not carried over into a more favorable attitude toward the minority group as a whole.

Case K, girl, 18, I.Q. 105, College, father a restaurant owner, West Virginia Methodist (Interview Method). Her initial anti-Jewish score was 22. It changed to 12 and remained at 7. She writes: "We discussed intermarriage; why people believe Jews are so clannish and why do college sororities and fraternities allow Catholics but do not allow Jews to enter them. I said, intermarriage depends upon the couple, if they can adjust their lives by doing so, then it is all right. Jews are so clannish because people make them so. If college organizations allow Catholics they should allow Jews."

Case L, girl, 17, I.Q. 104, 11th Grade, father deceased, small town, West Virginia Methodist (Interview Method). Her score was 24, changed to 15, and then to 5. She writes: "In Sunday School they try to tell us what the Jews believe. It is different from what the Rabbi's belief is. They are prejudiced against Rabbis. I and another girl take up for them very much since the one we had the experience with this past summer."

Case M, boy, 16, I.Q. 116, small town, father an insurance clerk, Connecticut Episcopal (Direct Group Method). His scores are 22, 14, and 6, changing from anti to pro-Jewish. He writes: "We talked over with the people who hadn't gone to the Conference the things discussed about the Jews. Fortunately, no one in this small town is race prejudiced, but it still opened their eyes to the situation. In our town, no one questions your race, color or religion, it's you personally that counts. If you're a good sport you are liked no matter what you are. I said I thought Jews should be given an equal place in any community. I reminded the group that Joseph, Mary, and Jesus were Jews and that we love them even though some of us forget that they were Jewish. I also reminded them that a great Church Day, Easter is celebrated because the Romans crucified Jesus calling him 'King of the Jews' because the Romans realized that he was a great Jewish man."

Case N, girl, 16, I.Q. 90, small town, father a metal finisher, Connecticut Episcopalian (Direct Group Method). Her scores were 30, 18, and 15 changing from anti-Jewish to the neutral range. She writes: "The discussion was about controlling wealth of the country and spoiling sections of the town where they live. I said, 'I think that too many people have prejudice against the Jewish people without any reasons for them.'"

Case O, girl, 16, I.Q. 125, father a real estate agent, small town, Connecticut Episcopalian (Direct Group Method). Her neutral score on the initial test was 16. In answering the question on whether the Rabbi's course changed her opinion she writes: "I think that he changed my entire opinion of the Jews. My family is anti-Jewish and I naturally was too. I thought they were rather inferior, clannish and wielded too much government power for a group without a nation." Her pro-Jewish score after the course was 2 and the stability score eight months later was 3. In the group discussions about Jews she writes: "We discussed the entire Jewish problem (?) in the state. The other people thought that Jews were no good, wielded too much power and as a people were inferior. They all had the feeling that Jews were stingy. I pointed out all the reasons that I could think of why they were wrong. Among them were: The Jews are becoming a problem because people like you treat them that way; and if the Jews do hold much power in the U.S. it is because they worked for it while the other so-called Americans lay down on the job."

Another report in the neutral attitude range is the Case of Q, girl, 18, High School Graduate, small town, her father a foreman, West Virginia Methodist (Direct Group Method). Her initial neutral score of 17 changed to 3 and went back to the neutral range of 10. She writes: "Our group has discussed the Jewish religion. We also discussed our attitudes toward Jews and their attitudes toward us. I was able to tell the group that the Jews had nothing against Christianity or Christians. I pointed out to them that certain Scriptures had meaning to those of the Jewish faith that Christians did not see. I told the group that Jews are human beings and should be treated as such. I pointed out that we do not treat a Catholic friend, a Baptist friend, or a Presbyterian friend any differently and we should not treat the Jew differently."

Another example of the favorable discussion of a respondent in the neutral range is the Case of R, girl, 17, I.Q. 116, her mother a high school teacher, large city, West Virginia Methodist (Direct Group Method). Her score was changed from 14 to 1 on the posttest and 2 on the stability test. She writes of discussions on "the wealth, the clannishness, the cheating-methods in business, intermarriage and the religion of the Jew." "Insofar as I was able and with the information that I had, I tried to defend the Jewish people. At times I was rather overcome by the majority against me."

On the other hand, we have two examples of unfavorable discussions of respondents in the neutral range even though they were subject to the Direct Group Method. Case S, boy, 18, I.Q. 124, large city, his father a grocer, West Virginia Methodist. His neutral score of 17 was lowered to 6, but on the stability test returned to 14. He writes: "Since I attend a school where there are a good many Jewish students (more than average) there naturally has been some discussion concerning the Jews. Since the majority of these Jews are from the Metropolitan area our discussion concerned our opinion of their manner and especially their dress. My general opinion is this: the way they dress is their business and as for their manner I wouldn't know because I avoid them whenever possible."

Case T, girl, 14, I.Q. 131, large city, her father a sales manager,

Connecticut Episcopalian. Her scores were raised from an initial 9 to 14 and 13 on the post-test and stability test. She writes: "I told some of my friends that I thought the Rabbi was trying to 'sell' us on Judaism. I think I was wrong. However, I do think many Jews while trying to clarify the question of Jewish persecution, present only their own side, emphasize it too much and give many people the impression I received, without meaning to. I think they are a bit too eager sometimes. One of my Jewish friends always remarks when you praise a person like Danny Kaye, 'Oh, he's Jewish you know!' Why does she always have to refer to the Jewishness of these important people. Is she ashamed of hers and wants to protect herself or cover it up this way? However, I think if the Psalms are studied more often in the Christian Church, the pupils would get a much better and broader view of how beautiful the Jewish religion is and how much alike Christians and Jews are. Before I never realized how beautiful and simple Judaism is and how it is fundamentally like ours. Before I thought of it as very sinister and mystical and weird." This last statement reminds us of the observations on this historical Christian belief about the mysteriousness of Judaism, made in the Introductory Chapter.

In the least prejudiced category on all three attitude tests, all the discussions reported by subjects taught by the Direct Group and Private Interview Methods are favorable. On the problem of immigration one said: "I said we should open our doors to the Jews." On resentment against Jewish students in the school, another reports, "I answered by telling of my experience with Jews. These have in all cases been among my richest experiences and associations." On the inferiority of Jews and their religion another reports, "I said that no religious sect is inferior. The world owes a great many things to the Jews and that the world wouldn't be what it is today from the viewpoint of religion if it had not been for the Jews. After all, our Blessed Lord was a Jew."

For a statistical examination, the respondents' own statements of their role in these discussions may be qualitatively divided into three categories: favorable toward the Jew, unfavorable toward the Jew, and mere factual statements about the course with the Rabbi. Fourteen in this third category were discarded in the statistical analysis.

To determine whether there is any statistical correlation between the scores in the attitude scale toward the Jew and the reported verbal behavior in group discussions about Jews, a contingency coefficient was calculated. The results in Table 27 indicate a small but significant degree of positive correlation between the respondents' attitude score and their verbal behavior in group discussions. The C is .28 with Pearson correction .34.

TABLE 27

CONTINGENCY COEFFICIENT BETWEEN ATTITUDE SCORES
AND VERBAL BEHAVIOR IN GROUP DISCUSSIONS

ATTITUDE SCORES ON THE POST-TEST	GROUP DISCUSSIONS ABOUT JEWS			
	Favorable	*Unfavorable*	*No Discussion*	*Totals*
Least Prejudiced	20	3	28	51
Neutral	12	2	36	50
Most Prejudiced	0	2	17	19
	32	7	81	120

When the chi square of the above table is computed according to the formula $X^2 = \dfrac{NC^2}{1 - C^2}$, the chi square is 14.23 which at four degrees of freedom is significant at the 1 percent level. This indicates that there is a significant positive association between degree of prejudice in the attitude scale and favorable or unfavorable verbal behavior in group discussions about Jews.

Furthermore, when the "no discussion" category is omitted in the calculation, the association between degree of prejudice and discussion about Jews in a group is significant. The chi square of the difference between favorable and unfavorable discussions and degree of prejudice is 9.55, significant below the 1 percent level (see Table 28).

TABLE 28

PERCENTAGE DISTRIBUTION OF THE VERBAL BEHAVIOR IN
GROUP DISCUSSIONS ABOUT JEWS OF RESPONDENTS
OF VARYING DEGREES OF PREJUDICE

Group Discussion	Least Prejudice	Neutral	Most Prejudice	Totals
Favorable	62.5	37.5	0	N = 32
Unfavorable	43.8	28.1	28.1	N = 7

As would be expected, Table 29 shows that those who were the least prejudiced in their scale score said they took part in group discussions about Jews much more frequently than did the most prejudiced. When the most prejudiced did record such discussions, their views were unfavorable toward the Jews, while the majority of the views expressed by the least prejudiced were favorable.

TABLE 29

PERCENTAGE DISTRIBUTION OF THE VERBAL BEHAVIOR OF THE
LEAST AND MOST PREJUDICED RESPONDENTS IN GROUP
DISCUSSIONS ABOUT JEWS (N73)

SCORE ON POST-TEST	Favorable	Unfavorable	No Discussion	Totals
Least Prejudiced	38.8	5.5	55.7	N = 54
Most Prejudiced	0	10.5	89.5	N = 19

The chi square is 8.66, significant at the 2 percent level.

When we analyze the verbal behavior in group discussions about Jews of the respondents whose attitude score toward the Jew was improved by the Rabbi's course, as compared with the respondents whose attitude score did not change, we find no significant statistical difference in verbal behavior (see Table 30).

The chi square is 3.26, significant at the 20 percent level. We may only say that there is a slight tendency on the part of the whole group that changed in attitude to participate more frequently in favorable discussions about Jews.

However, a breakdown of the reported discussions about Jews as they are related by the least prejudiced, the neutral, and the most prejudiced scorers does reveal a statistically significant difference for the neutrals' verbal behavior.

TABLE 30

PERCENTAGE DISTRIBUTION OF THE VERBAL BEHAVIOR IN THE "NO CHANGE IN ATTITUDE" AND THOSE WHO FALL IN THE "CHANGE IN ATTITUDE" GROUPS (N120)

TOTAL ATTITUDE SCORE ON POST-TEST	GROUP DISCUSSIONS ABOUT JEWS			
	Favorable	*Unfavorable*	*No Discussion*	*Totals*
Group I No Change in Attitude	20.4	3.7	76.3	N = 54
Groups II and III Change in Attitude	31.8	7.6	60.6	N = 66

The neutrals subject to the Direct Group and Focused Private Interview Methods show a much greater tendency to participate favorably in group discussions about Jews than do the neutrals subject to the Indirect Method which did not change attitudes. The chi square is 12.5, significant at below the 1 percent level (see Table 31).

TABLE 31

PERCENTAGE DISTRIBUTION OF VERBAL BEHAVIOR IN DISCUSSIONS ABOUT JEWS OF RESPONDENTS WHO FALL IN THE NEUTRAL SCORE RANGE IN THE ATTITUDE SCALE (N50)

NEUTRAL ATTITUDE SCORE ON POST-TEST	GROUP DISCUSSIONS ABOUT JEWS		
	Favorable	*Unfavorable*	*No Discussion*
Groups I, Conn. and W.Va. No Attitude Change	7.4	0	92.6 (N27)
Groups II and III, Conn. and W.Va. Attitude Changed	43.5	8.6	47.9 (N23)

Of all the respondents subject to the Indirect Group Method who report discussions about Jews, 20.4 percent indicate favorable participation, 3.7 percent unfavorable, and 75.9 percent no participation. Of all the respondents subject to the Direct Group and Private Interview Methods reporting discussions, 31.8 percent indicate favorable participation, 7.6 percent unfavorable, and 60.6 percent no participation. There is, however, a significant difference in the neutral range, as indicated in Table 31. For the sampling in this neutral category, we may say that there is greater probability that those whose attitudes have been effectively changed, will participate favorably in group discussion about Jews more frequently than will those in whom the Indirect Teaching Method produced no change.

In connection with this inference, it may also be observed that it was only the neutrals who showed a statistically significant difference as between those subject to the Indirect Group and those subject to either the Direct Group or Private Interview Methods on Question 2 of the Information Sheet. Eight months after the courses, the respondents indicated whether the course with the Rabbi changed their opinion about Jews. On this question, "Did the Rabbi's course change any opinions you may have had about Jews? Yes— No—" there was no significant difference between the least prejudiced subjects nor any difference between the most prejudiced subject in any of the three methods. However, as between the neutrals taught by the Indirect Group Method and the neutrals taught by the Direct Group and Private Interview Methods which did produce change in attitudes, there is in Question 2 a chi square of 3.86, or a difference significant at the 5 percent level (see Table 32).

From a study of these reported discussions, we observe first a validation of the attitude scale itself. The attitude scores of the most prejudiced and the least prejudiced on the scale are confirmed by the unfavorable and favorable nature of their own respective reports. The first case reported, Case A, is a rather dramatic corroboration of the statistical findings regarding the Indirect Group Method. While it increases an appreciation of the Jewish contribu-

TABLE 32

PERCENTAGE DISTRIBUTION OF RESPONDENTS SUBJECT TO DIFFER-
ENT TEACHING METHODS WHO DECLARED OPINIONS WERE
CHANGED BY THE RABBI'S COURSE

Score on Post-Test	Method	Opinion Changed	No Change	Totals
Least Prejudiced	Indirect	41.2	58.8	N17
Least Prejudiced	Direct and Interview	52.5	47.5	N40

(The chi square .61 is significant only at the 40 percent level.)

Neutrals	Indirect	60.0	40.0	N30
Neutrals	Direct and Interview	77.8	22.2	N28

(The chi square 3.86 is significant at the 5 percent level.)

Most Prejudiced	Indirect	8.3	91.7	N12
Most Prejudiced	Direct and Interview	14.2	85.8	N7

(The chi square .16 is significant only at the 90 percent level.)

tion to Christianity, the Indirect Group Method does not change prejudice against Jews. These taught by the Direct Group and Private Focused Interview Methods who initially scored in the most prejudiced range and then lowered their scores to the neutral range on the Post-Test (Cases I, J, K, L, M, and N), give favorable discussion reports. This confirms the statistical findings regarding the greater degree of favorable participation in discussions about Jews on the part of the neutrals subject to the Direct Group and Private Interview Methods as compared to neutrals subject to the Indirect Group Method. The Case of J is an interesting exception. He gives an ambivalent report (see page 81). It should be noted that in his stability test his new neutral score went back to his original anti-Jewish score. Case J was taught by the Private Interview Method. The report of his interview is given in Chapter II. That interview shows his personal unhappiness about purchasing a blue instead of a tan suit because the latter was too expensive. It will be recalled that J blames this on the Jews. His stability test score of 31 and his reported discussion about Jews would lead us to believe that his personal disappointment was too deep to be resolved by a single interview.

Though there are two cases in the neutral category which reveal a "boomerang" result (Case R and Case S), all the other neutral scorers in the Direct Group and Private Interview Methods who report discussions, describe them as favorable toward Jews, confirming the statistical findings in this regard.

From the statistical analysis of the reported discussions, we conclude that there is a small but significant positive correlation between the degree of one's prejudice and the verbal behavior of that person in group discussions about Jews. The least prejudiced show a greater percentage of behavior favorable to Jews in these discussions. The highest percentage of those who do not even participate in such discussions is among the most prejudiced, 89.5 percent. Those in the neutral score range show the highest percentage of the respondents who declare the Rabbi's course changed their opinions. In this neutral group, those taught by the Direct Group and Focused Private Interview Methods which change attitude show a greater percentage of participation in group discussions favorable to the Jew than do those taught by the Indirect Group Method which produced no change in attitude.

VERBAL BEHAVIOR IN ANTI-JEWISH SITUATIONS

On question 4 of the Information Sheet, of 137 respondents 61 or 44.5 percent report that they witnessed anti-Jewish incidents or heard anti-Jewish remarks during the eight months following the course with the Rabbi. Seventy-three respondents or 54.5 percent report no anti-Jewish experience. It is interesting to note that while 47.2 percent of the least prejudiced and 50.1 percent of the neutrals report witnessing anti-Jewish situations, only 35.2 percent of the most prejudiced make such a report. We may well ask whether the most prejudiced refrain from recording anti-Jewish situations because they are not conscious of the prejudice in the situation or whether the most prejudiced hesitate to have their behavior in such situations exposed, since the few most prejudiced who do report such situations, support the hostility toward Jews expressed in these situations?

Of the 61 reporting anti-Jewish situations, 59 describe the anti-Jewish situation, record what they thought about it and state what they did, if anything, in the situation. A few examples of anti-Jewish situations as described by the respondents will be presented here.

The following respondents did do something to defend the Jew. Case P; (attitudes scores 1, 0, 1) writes: "One of my friends' mother gave her opinion on Jews, the usual, 'O, I like them but they do know how to "jew" you down, etc.' Perhaps I should have said more than I did. I disagreed as politely as I could but afraid it didn't change her attitude." Case 2 (attitude scores 18, 9, 6), "I have heard it said that Hitler had the right idea about getting rid of the Jews. It made me very angry and I tried to argue it down but we both got angry and it didn't do any good." Case 3 (attitude scores 4, 2, 1), "Someone mentioned the fact that they knew a Jew who shot someone and someone else said that it was to be expected as all Jews were sneaky, filthy, murderous people. I thought it very indecent, unfair, unnecessary, definitely untruthful, and showed no fair play at all. I said that no one sect had the majority of sinful people, that it depends on the individual, not on race or creed as to what kind of person they are." Case 4 (attitude scores 7, 3, 0), "A girl friend described a girl we had just met to someone else. She said she did not like her—that she was Jewish; this with a facial expression insinuating that being Jewish, how could you like her. I was rather disappointed with my friend. I said that I liked the girl, she was very nice." Case I (attitudes scores 36, 12, 7): "We were playing basketball when one boy said, 'I would not play with a rotten Jew if he came to this school, I would quit the team fast.' I thought the remark was uncalled for. I told him he had his wires crossed and that if the boy could play, let him, and you play with him." Case 6 (attitudes scores 8, 1, 4): "A friend of mine and I were walking up the street one day when two women came toward us. My friend said, 'Here comes two old Kikes, who live near us—just ignore them.' I thought it was a mean remark. People's feelings are hurt by just such things. I said 'hello' to the women and 'goodbye' to my friend."

The following respondents did not say anything to defend the Jew. Case 1 (attitudes scores 0, 1, 1): "I once heard several people ridiculing the Jewish religion, berating Jews for having so many holidays separate from ours and claiming that some Jews work on Sunday just so they can make money from other faiths. I think these remarks are unfair and narrow minded. The people were so busily engaged in their conversation that I thought it would be futile to say anything." Case 2 (attitude scores 18, 6, 7): "I would rather not write the remark down. It was very un-American. I said nothing." Case 3 (attitude scores 9, 6, 5): "Referring to the Palestinian conflict someone said he hoped they killed all the Jews—we would be rid of the money-grabbing devils! To me this statement was banal, trite, and even ignorant. I hope there are not many like him. I did not answer him." Case 4 (attitude scores 8, 6, 7): "A woman who is a member of the D.A.R. and head of a Youth Hostel made a remark to the effect that three of the boys staying at the hostel were 'damn New York Jews.' I feel that a woman in that position has no right to make such a statement. I was told that the boys later defended themselves." Case 5 (attitudes score 7, 2, 4): "The remark was made over the rudeness and bad manners of Jews on the subway. I feel none of us are at our best on the subway, all people have their faults. (Said nothing.)" Case 6 (attitudes score 8, 11, 12): "Several people said the Jews are clannish and have no honor code in business. I thought they were prejudiced. I disagreed but felt there was no use in saying anything." Case J (attitudes scores 35, 19, 31): "About a jewelry merchant and what a cheat he was. I thought it to be the fault of the person who made the remark. I said nothing because I would have spoken too far out of turn if I had." Case 8 (attitude scores 19, 23, 22): "I have been told that the Jews are tight with their money. Though some may be this way I have received many nice gifts from Jews I know. I didn't say anything. I do not like to join in such criticism in conversation."

In order to make a statistical analysis of these 59 reports, the respondents' actions are arranged in the following categories. What the respondent *thought* about the anti-Jewish situation is qualitatively divided according to whether the respondent supports group hostility, opposes group hostility, or is neutral in his attitude. What the respondent *did* in the situation is qualitatively divided into verbal action or inaction.

To determine whether there is any correlation between the scores in the attitude scale and the reported verbal action or inaction in anti-Jewish situations, a contingency coefficient was calculated. The results in Table 33 indicate very little correlation between attitude scores and action in anti-Jewish situations. The C is .173; with a Pearson correction it is .21.

TABLE 33

CONTINGENCY COEFFICIENT BETWEEN ATTITUDE SCORES AND
VERBAL BEHAVIOR IN ANTI-JEWISH SITUATIONS

Attitude Score on Post-Test	Verbal Action	Inaction	No Situation	Totals
Least Prejudiced	16	10	29	55
Neutral	13	14	33	60
Most Prejudiced	1	5	14	20
	30	29	76	135

When the chi square of the above table is computed according to the formula $X^2 = \dfrac{NC^2}{1 - C^2}$, the chi square is 4.17. At four degrees of freedom, this is significant only at about the 40 percent level. There is, then, no positive association between the degree of prejudice in the attitude scale and verbal action or inaction in anti-Jewish situations.

When the "no situation" category is omitted, the association between the degree of prejudice and action or inaction in anti-Jewish situations is again not statistically significant though the least prejudiced show a greater tendency toward verbal action in such situations. Table 34 shows the percentage. The chi square is 4.07 significant above the 10 percent level.

TABLE 34

PERCENTAGE DISTRIBUTION OF THE VERBAL ACTION IN
ANTI-JEWISH SITUATIONS OF RESPONDENTS OF
VARYING DEGREE OF PREJUDICE

	Least Prejudiced	*Neutral*	*Most Prejudiced*	*Total*
Verbal Action	53.3	43.3	3.4	N30
Inaction	34.5	48.6	16.9	N29

While there is no significant statistical correlation between action in anti-Jewish situations and scores on the attitude scale, we note that 79.8 percent of the total respondents state on the Information Sheet that they disliked the anti-Jewish incident or remark and declared their opposition to the hostility expressed in the situation. However, 57.6 percent of the total respondents said nothing in these situations to refute the charges against the Jews. While the greater percentage disliked the situation, the greater percentage said nothing about it. A qualitative comparison of these respondents' attitude and their behavior in the anti-Jewish situations they described is given in Table 35.

TABLE 35

PERCENTAGE DISTRIBUTION OF THE RESPONDENTS VERBAL
BEHAVIOR AND ATTITUDE IN ANTI-JEWISH
SITUATIONS (N59)

WHAT DID YOU SAY?	WHAT DID YOU THINK ABOUT THE SITUATION?			
	Supports Group Hostility	*Opposes Group Hostility*	*Neutral*	*Totals*
Verbal Action	1.6	40.7		42.3
Inaction	10.2	38.9	8.6	57.7

The chi square of 6.88 is significant at the 4 percent level. We may be reasonably sure that this group shows a greater degree of verbal inaction than verbal action in their behavior in anti-Jewish situations. Of the 47 who disliked the hostility expressed toward the

Jews only 24 said something to defend the Jews in the situations.

Item 10 in the attitude scale reads: "People who are not Jewish should try to answer those who say things against the Jews." Those most prejudiced on the initial attitude tests show greater disagreement and those least prejudiced show greater agreement with item 10. Forty-two percent of the highest quartile of all the groups combined (N477) "Disagree" and 19 percent "Slightly Disagree," while 76 percent of the lowest quartile "Agree" and 9 percent "Slightly Agree." The distribution of the responses on this item are shown in Table 36.

TABLE 36

PERCENTAGE DISTRIBUTION OF RESPONSES OF THE MOST
PREJUDICED AND THE LEAST PREJUDICED ON ITEM
10 ON INITIAL TEST (TOTAL N477)

	Agree	Slightly Agree	Slightly Disagree	Disagree	Totals
Most Prejudiced	21.9	16.4	19.5	42.2	128 (N)
Least Prejudiced	76.8	8.8	5.6	8.8	125 (N)

As regards the most prejudiced, it is also of interest to note that while the majority of the most prejudiced recognize the contribution which the Jews have made to religion (item 14 in the scale), they are, nonetheless, opposed to defending the contemporary Jews. In Table 37 may be seen the percentage of agreement and disagreement of the most prejudiced on items 10 and 14.

TABLE 37

PERCENTAGE COMPARISON OF THE RESPONSES OF THE MOST
PREJUDICED ON ITEMS 10 AND 14 (HIGHEST
QUARTILE N128)

	Agreement (0 and 1)	Disagreement (2 and 3)
Item 14 Jews Contribute to Religion	60	40
Item 10 Answer Charges against Jews	39	61

We found in Chapter III that while the most prejudiced increased their knowledge of Jewish contributions to Christianity by the Indirect Group Teaching Method, this still did not decrease their prejudice against Jews. We can now add that they also continued their opposition to any defense of the Jew.

The following table (Table 38) gives the distribution of the responses on item 10 of the Attitude Scale of those in all the experimental groups who returned the Information Sheet.

TABLE 38

PERCENTAGE DISTRIBUTION OF THE RESPONSES ON ITEM
10 OF THE SCALE OF SUBJECTS RETURNING
INFORMATION SHEET (N137)

	AGREEMENT		DISAGREEMENT	
	Agree	*Slightly Agree*	*Slightly Disagree*	*Disagree*
I. Conn. Episcopal Indirect (N45)				
Test	44.4	6.6	15.5	33.5
Post-Test	33.5	22.2	26.6	17.7
Stability Test	40.0	28.8	17.7	13.5
II. Conn. Episcopal Direct (N38)				
Test	42.1	23.7	10.5	23.7
Post-Test	52.6	23.7	10.5	13.2
Stability Test	52.6	26.4	10.5	10.5
I. W.Va. Methodist Indirect (N15)				
Test	40.0	26.7	13.3	20.0
Post-Test	33.3	26.7	20.0	20.0
Stability Test	26.6	33.3	26.7	13.3
II. W.Va. Methodist Interview (N22)				
Test	45.5	31.8	9.1	13.7
Post-Test	40.9	27.3	27.3	4.5
Stability Test	86.3	13.7	—	—
III. W.Va. Methodist Direct (N17)				
Test	58.8	11.8	5.9	23.5
Post-Test	64.7	29.4	5.9	—
Stability Test	70.5	11.8	11.8	—

Table 38 indicates that the higher percentages of all experimental groups throughout all three tests agree with the opinion that charges made against the Jew *should* be answered.

Of the 59 respondents who report witnessing anti-Jewish situations, 36 agreed on the post-test with item 10 on the attitude scale that remarks against Jews should be answered. Nonetheless, in such situations which they describe only 44 percent state that they actually defended the Jew. Table 39 presents a qualitative analysis of the relation between the verbal attitude toward and the actual verbal behavior in anti-Jewish situations of those respondents who agreed on the attitude scale that such charges against Jews should be answered.

TABLE 39

PERCENTAGE DISTRIBUTION OF THE VERBAL BEHAVIOR OF
RESPONDENTS IN ANTI-JEWISH SITUATIONS WHO AGREED
WITH ITEM 10 ON THE ATTITUDE SCALE (N36)

WHAT DID YOU SAY?	WHAT DID YOU THINK ABOUT THE SITUATION?			
	Support Hostility	*Oppose Hostility*	*Neutral*	*Totals*
Verbal Action	0	44.4		44.4
Inaction	8.3	38.8	8.3	55.4

The chi square 5.76 is significant at the 5 percent level. We may be reasonably sure that though this group declares that charges against Jews should be answered, the verbal behavior of the majority of the members of the group in anti-Jewish situations is one of inaction.

What is the behavior in anti-Jewish situations of all those who fall in the least prejudiced category after the various courses. According to Table 40, these least prejudiced show a greater tendency to answer charges against Jews than do the most prejudiced. The chi square is 4.08 significant at the 10 percent level.

What is the behavior in anti-Jewish situations of all those who fall in the group which showed a group change in attitude on the total score of the scale as compared to those who fall in the group which showed no group change in attitude? Table 41 shows no significant difference between the two groups in reacting to anti-Jewish situations. The chi square is .98 significant only at the 60 percent level.

TABLE 40

PERCENTAGE DISTRIBUTION OF THE VERBAL BEHAVIOR OF RE-
SPONDENTS IN ANTI-JEWISH SITUATIONS WHO FALL IN
THE LEAST PREJUDICED AND MOST PREJUDICED
CATEGORIES IN THE ATTITUDE SCALE (N76)

Post-Test Score	Verbal Action	Inaction	No Incident	Totals
Least Prejudiced	29.1	18.1	52.8	N55
Most Prejudiced	5.8	29.4	64.8	N21

TABLE 41

PERCENTAGE DISTRIBUTION OF VERBAL BEHAVIOR IN ANTI-
JEWISH SITUATIONS OF RESPONDENTS WHO FALL IN
THE "CHANGE" AND "NO CHANGE IN ATTITUDE"
CATEGORIES (N134)

	Verbal Action	Inaction	No Incident	Total
Attitude Not Changed: Groups I, Conn. and W.Va.	22.0	27.1	50.9	N59
Attitude Changed: Groups II and III, Conn. and W.Va.	22.3	20.0	57.7	N75

There is no statistical basis for concluding, therefore, that the group which changed its attitude by the better teaching methods differed in its verbal behavior in actual anti-Jewish situations from the group which did not change its attitude.

Of the 22 respondents who report both participation in group discussions about Jews and witnessing anti-Jewish situations, all 22 report their roles as favorable to Jews in discussions, but only 11 of these report verbal defense of Jews in the face of anti-Jewish situations. Only 50 percent of those who participate favorably in group discussions about Jews also defend the Jew in anti-Jewish situations.

With reference to behavior in actual anti-Jewish situations, we conclude that there is no positive correlation between the respondent's degree of prejudice and his verbal action in defending Jews in anti-Jewish situations. While the least prejudiced show a slight tendency to be more verbally active than inactive in these situations, the group as a whole shows a greater degree of inaction than action in anti-Jewish situations. Of those who in the attitudes scale declare charges against Jews *should* be answered the majority are, nonetheless, inactive verbally in anti-Jewish situations. Furthermore, more favorable changes in attitudes toward Jews brought about by the more effective teaching methods did not alter this general pattern of verbal inaction in the face of anti-Jewish incidents or remarks.

As regards group discussions about Jews, we conclude that there is a small but significant positive correlation between the degree of one's prejudice toward the Jew and one's favorable participation in group discussions about the Jew. The least prejudiced, as would be expected, show a greater degree of participation in such discussions. In this regard there is no difference in degree of participation as to whether the least prejudiced were taught by the Indirect Group or the Direct Group and Private Interview Methods for changing attitudes. However, in the neutral range on the attitude scores toward the Jew, whether the "neutrals" were taught by the Indirect or by the Direct and Interview Methods does make a difference in the degree of their participation in group discussions about Jews. Those of the "neutrals" whose attitudes were changed by the Direct Group and Focused Private Interview Methods show a significantly greater degree of favorable participation in group discussions about Jews than do those "neutrals" whose attitudes were left unchanged by the Indirect Group Method. This relation of verbal behavior to method of changing attitude among the neutrals is also significant because among all three degrees of prejudice, the "neutrals" were the highest in percentage who declared the Rabbi's course changed their opinions. Among the "neutrals" in whom the Direct Group and Private Interview Methods produced the greatest change in attitude, there was a significant greater degree of favorable participation in group discussions about Jews.

The verbal behavior of the respondents in anti-Jewish situations presents a different picture. There is no positive association between the degree of one's prejudice and one's favorable verbal action in face of anti-Jewish incidents or remarks. The majority in all groups on item 10 of the attitudes scale—the least prejudiced, the neutrals, as well as the most prejudiced in attitude toward the Jew—declare that charges against the Jew should be answered. Indeed of the total number who actually report anti-Jewish incidents 79.8 percent declared that they "thought" the anti-Jewish incident "un-Christian," "un-American," "unfair," "uncalled for," etc., etc. However, of this total number reporting dislike for anti-Jewish incidents, only 42.4 percent stated that they said something to refute the charges against the Jew. And only 44 percent of those who also declared on the attitudes scale that charges should be answered did so in actual situations. The least prejudiced show a slight tendency to be more verbally active in defending Jews in anti-Jewish situations; but the group as a whole, irrespective of whether the group's attitude toward Jews was changed or not, show a greater degree of inaction than favorable verbal action in anti-Jewish situations.

THE SUPERIORITY OF THE DIRECT GROUP METHOD

It is logical to inquire why the least prejudiced and those who improved their attitude toward the Jew do not behave in the anti-Jewish situations they witness as they behave in their group discussions about Jews. We may suggest four factors to account for this difference in verbal behavior. Firstly, the situations differ in kind. In group discussions about Jews, as the respondents themselves describe them, there is an intellectual exchange of ideas about the Jews, their religion and customs, as well as their problems in America. In anti-Jewish situations there is an emotional content frequently charged with high tension. The respondent is willing to participate in intellectual discussions about Jews and was even helped by the information received from the course with the Rabbi to do so favorably toward the Jew. However, like most people in similar situations, the respondent is not inclined to become actively involved in an unpleasant attack on a third party.

Secondly, most of the group discussions took place in church youth groups in which the respondent is a member. He has a sense of belonging to the group. Furthermore, because he attended the Seminar, the respondent was a leader in this group in which he already enjoyed approval and status. There was little risk of losing this position by favorable participation in an intellectual discussion about the Jew. In the anti-Jewish situation, the respondent is not prepared to face disapproval or loss of status which might occur if he defended the Jew in an unstructured group of strangers or before his elders or even before his own peers. It must be remembered that the respondents are adolescents about 16 years of age where the need for adult approval and security is great.

Thirdly, from the answers reported by those who defended the Jew in anti-Jewish situations we observe that these answers range from timidity to belligerency; that almost all state that their defense had no influence; and that the respondents doubt whether they handled the situation effectively. Also those who state they disapproved the anti-Jewish remark but did not say anything about it, add that they did not know what to say, and like most people in similar situations imply that an answer was not morally or socially required of them. There may well be less participation in defending the Jew in anti-Jewish situations, even on the part of the least prejudiced, simply because they do not know how to enter into these situations and be effective. In addition to the risk of disapproval, there is the lack of technique, which handicaps the least prejudiced in their verbal defense of the Jews.

Finally, personality factors, such as whether the respondent is extraversial or intraversial, must be taken into consideration in analyzing why the respondent did or did not take verbal action in witnessing an anti-Jewish situation.

While certain courses taken by the respondents with the Rabbi changed their attitudes and helped them in group discussions, these courses did not prepare the respondents in methods for defending the Jew in anti-Jewish situations, nor did these courses advise them whether an aggressive or persuasive, an emotional or intellectual approach is the more effective way in handling such situations.[1] Of course, the main purpose of this study in changing attitudes by effective methods was to decrease the tendency of the respondents themselves to make anti-Semitic remarks.

The opposite findings on the relation of verbal behavior to change in attitude toward the Jews in the two different types of behavior—group discussion about Jews and anti-Jewish situations —lends support to the dynamic influence of the group on the individual or to the "field theory of personality." The individual's positive attitude as well as his favorable verbal behavior toward the Jews are most effectively conditioned by his experiences in a group to which he belongs and which gives him his status and set of values. In Chapter IV we observed that the Direct Group Method was more effective than the Focused Private Interview Method in changing the degree of prejudice of the group toward the Jew, because the change was reinforced by group approval. In Chapter V we found that once the attitude was changed, it was more stable among those who were involved with their own group in the Rabbi's guided group discussion of attitudes toward the Jew. We accounted for the fact that the changed attitude of this group did not fluctuate eight months later as did the attitude of those who had one interview with the Rabbi by suggesting that the individual members in the Direct Group Method had had their new attitudes anchored in group approval, whereas the attitude of the others did fluctuate because they could refer their new attitude only to an interview with a Rabbi not a member of their own group. Now, in Chapter VI, we discover, further, that the favorable change in attitude resulting from the Direct Group teaching method is verbally expressed more frequently in group discussions about Jews

[1] Claire Selltiz et al., "The Acceptability of Answers to Anti-Semitic Remarks," *International Journal of Opinion and Attitude Research,* vol. 4, no. 3, 1950, pp. 353–90.

than is the change in attitude resulting from the individual interview. Furthermore, this favorable verbal behavior occurs more frequently in the kind of group experience in which the individual has status than it does in experiences in which the individual enjoys no group-structured support. To repeat the quotation from Kurt Lewin stated in Chapter I: "only by anchoring his own conduct in something as large, substantial, and supra-individual as the culture of a group can the individual stabilize his new beliefs sufficiently to keep them immune from the day-by-day fluctuations of mood and influences."

VII. SUMMARY AND CONCLUSION

THIS has been an experiment in interfaith education designed to reduce the prejudice of Christians toward Jews. It is the first time that methods for changing the attitudes of Christians toward Jews have been subjected to scientific experimentation in a religious setting in which the participants have been Christians and a Rabbi. That religion—specifically the close religious interrelationship that exists between Christianity and Judaism—functions as a vital factor in the development of hostility between Christian and Jew has been postulated in the Introduction to this study. Not only the role of religion in *creating* anti-Jewish feelings but also the potentialities within religion for *reducing* these prejudices is an important assumption in this experiment.

At present the most popular method used in religious education to reduce anti-Jewish prejudice is one in which Jew or Christian presents historical facts about the significant Jewish contributions to Christianity. They emphasize the fact that Christian and Jew share the religious values of the Bible and profess together common moral and spiritual principles. This technique is widely employed by both Jewish and Christian advocates of "good will." On the basis of certain psychological theories, outlined in the Introduction, the supposition may be made that increasing a Christian's knowledge of the Jewish origins of his religion could act as a boomerang and actually reinforce his anti-Jewish prejudices. To test whether the knowledge and the acceptance of the Jewish origins of Christianity reduces or increases anti-Jewish attitudes has been a major interest of this controlled experiment.

The method by which Christians learn about the Jewish contributions to Christianity and about the religious ideals which Jews and Christians possess in common has been defined here as the Indirect Group Method. In this experiment it is described as a four-dimensional approach. (1) The specific information is transmitted to Christians under favorable conditions which include (2) friendly association between the Christian students and their instructor who is a Rabbi, an official representative of Judaism. The Rabbi enjoys (3) prestige which stems from being authorized by the Christian Church to teach its students. The stimulus material in the course for changing anti-Jewish attitudes is (4) emotional as well as informational since it is Biblical material which possesses emotional valence for Church members. This fourfold method is called Indirect because no direct reference is made by the Jewish instructor to specific anti-Jewish prejudices nor are the Christian students encouraged to speak of their own experiences with Jews or of their attitudes toward Jews.

The results of the application of this Indirect Group Method to the Christian groups were tested and compared with the results of two other methods employed in this experiment for changing the attitude of Christian toward Jew. One is called here the Direct Group Method. In addition to the four dimensions of the Indirect Method, the Direct Group Method includes the dynamic participation of the Christian students as a group, together with their Jewish instructor, in a direct group discussion of anti-Jewish attitudes. The Christian students are deliberately involved in the problem of Christian-Jewish relations; misinformation about the contemporary Jew is corrected by the Jewish instructor, and most important, and as a kind of group catharsis of hostility, is the opportunity given the Christian students to express and evaluate their experiences with and their attitude toward the Jews.

The third method is called the Focused Private Interview. In this approach the four-dimensional Indirect Method is employed in the class. However, in addition each individual member of the group is interviewed privately by the Rabbi and encouraged to relate his personal experiences with Jews. During this interview misinformation about the contemporary Jew is corrected; opportunity is given to the Christian student for expression of hostility toward the Jew either directly or by projection; and effort is made to reorient the thinking of the Christian student in terms of new values about the Jew.

This interfaith educational experiment which tested the results of these three methods took place in the summer of 1946 when the Rabbi was invited to teach the Book of Psalms to members of the Episcopal Diocese of Connecticut assembled from many communities in that state, and in the summer of 1947 when the Rabbi was invited to teach the Old Testament to members of the Methodist Church assembled from many communities in the state of West Virginia. The total number of Protestant students involved in this experiment was 525. Their average age was 16. The control group was made up of 357 students who received no instruction. Of this number, 309 answered all items in the several tests. In the experimental groups, two classes of 49 and 21 students each were subjected to the Indirect Group Method; two classes of 48 and 25 students each were conducted by the Direct Group Method; and each member of one class of 25 students was given a Focused Private Interview with the Rabbi. The same Rabbi conducted all five experimental classes. All the students were given, by Christian officials of the Seminars, two forms of an attitudes test one week apart to measure their attitude toward the Jew. To the 168 students in the experimental groups the two forms were administered before and after the courses of study with the Rabbi; and a third form was distributed eight months later by mail to determine the stability of the change in attitude. In addition, to investigate the relation of change in attitude toward the Jew to verbal behavior in actual situations involving Jews, an Information Questionnaire was mailed eight months later to the members of the experimental groups to get a record of their verbal behavior both in group discussions about Jews and as witnesses to anti-Jewish incidents or remarks.

For the attitudes test, a scale for measuring attitude toward the

Jew containing 16 items was prepared. A correlation of .85 on two forms of the scale administered to 309 uninstructed students who answered all the items in the scale gives a high degree of reliability to the scale. (Applying the odd-even split half technique to one form of the scale administered to five groups totaling 406 also gives high correlations ranging from .82 to .89.) The scale also satisfies the criterion of internal consistency. With the exception of only one item, number 15, the discriminating powers of each item, ranging from .8 to 2.16, indicates that the scale adequately discriminates between the least and the most prejudiced. The validity of the items is confirmed by the study of Levinson-Sanford. Thirteen of the items in the scale of this study are closely related to similar statements in the Levinson-Sanford "Scale for the Measurement of Anti-Semitism." Further qualitative corroboration of the validity of the items was found in the 25 personal interviews conducted by the Rabbi and in the reports of the 137 respondents in the Information Questionnaire. The scoring range of the scale is from 0 to 48. In this experiment the lowest quartile ranged from 0 to 9 and were described as pro-Jewish; scores of 22–42 fell in the highest quartile and were termed anti-Jewish; scores in the 2d and 3d quartile ranged from 10 to 21 and were considered "neutrals."

The majority of the 477 Christians who answered all items in the test were initially neither pro-Jewish nor anti-Jewish. They were in the neutral category. According to the initial test, 26.8 percent were anti-Jewish, 51.0 percent neutral, and 26.2 percent more or less pro-Jewish.

THE RESULTS OF THE METHODS FOR CHANGING
ATTITUDE TOWARD THE JEW

The Indirect Group Method, which teaches the Jewish origins of and contributions to Christianity and the religio-democratic values of the Bible shared by Christian and Jew alike, does *not* change the attitude of Christian toward the Jew. This method does *not* decrease the degree of prejudice toward the Jew. If it is any consolation, it may be noted that this popular interfaith technique does not *increase* anti-Jewish prejudice.

As a result of the Indirect Group Method, the Christians increase their knowledge of as well as their acceptance of the fact that they "are indebted to the Jews for their contribution to religion." This includes even the most prejudiced Christians. However, this knowledge does not improve the attitude of the Christians as a group toward the Jew. The mean score of the Christian group on the attitudes test toward the Jew before such an indirect interfaith approach remains substantially the same afterwards.

A significant change in the attitude of Christian toward Jew *is* brought about by the Direct Group Method. A Christian group does lower its mean score in the attitudes scale and becomes more favorable toward the Jew, if it is guided to participate in direct discussions of the Christian's personal experiences with and attitudes toward the Jew. This Direct Group Method stimulates group involvement in the Christian-Jewish problem; corrects misinformation about contemporary Jews; affords a group catharsis for hostility; and gives an opportunity for a reorientation of values in relation to the Jew.

A more favorable attitude toward the Jew on the part of Christians results from a private interview which is focused on contemporary Christian-Jewish relations. The mean score of a Christian group is lowered and the prejudice of the group toward the Jew decreases when each individual member is privately interviewed by a Rabbi who encourages him to speak freely of his experiences with Jews and helps him to achieve better insight into his relations with Jews.

The favorable changes in the attitude of Christians toward the Jew which result from effective teaching methods are maintained. The lowered mean score on the attitudes test of those Christian groups subject to the Direct Group Method and the Focused Private Interview remains stable eight months later. On the other hand, the mean score on the attitudes test of those Christians taught by the Indirect Group Method is slightly higher eight months later, though not enough to indicate an increase in anti-Jewish prejudice.

The Direct Group Method is more effective than the Focused Private Interview in changing the attitude of Christians toward the Jew. The mean score of the Christian group on the attitudes scale is lowered more by the Direct Group Method than it is lowered by the Focused Private Interview. Furthermore, the change in the attitude of Christians resulting from the Direct Group Method is more stable eight months later than it is in the case of the Focused Private Interview.

It will be recalled that in the case of a few individuals whose scores were extremely anti-Jewish, the cathartic effect of either the Direct Group Method or of the Private Interview was insufficient to alter their attitudes. It appears that something more penetrating and extensive than the short sessions this experiment afforded is necessary to change the minds of those whose attitudes are *extremely* anti-Jewish.

THE RESULTS OF THE VERBAL BEHAVIOR OF CHRISTIANS IN GROUP DISCUSSIONS ABOUT JEWS

There is a small but significant correlation between the attitude of a Christian toward the Jew and his verbal behavior in discussions about Jews, in groups in which the Christian has status and a feeling of belonging.

The least prejudiced Christians participate the most frequently and the most favorably in such group discussions about Jews.

The majority of the Christians neutral in their attitude toward the Jew who report group discussion about Jews indicate their own role to be favorable toward the Jew.

The most prejudiced Christians report the fewest such group discussions in proportion to their number and when they do report such discussions, their own role is unfavorable toward the Jew.

The Direct Group and Private Interview Teaching Methods which change the attitude of the majority of the Christians (the neutrals on the initial test), will also stimulate more frequent favorable participation among these Christians in group discussion about Jews than will be found among the neutral Christians subject to the influence of the Indirect Group Method.

A higher percentage of the majority of Christians (the neutrals on the initial test) declare their opinion about Jews to have been changed when they were influenced by the Direct Group and the Focused Private Interview Methods.

THE RESULTS IN THE VERBAL BEHAVIOR OF CHRISTIANS
WHO WITNESS ANTI-JEWISH SITUATIONS

There is no association between the degree of prejudice of a Christian toward the Jew and his verbal behavior in witnessing anti-Jewish situations.

Regardless of whether their attitude toward the Jew is favorable or unfavorable, there is a higher degree of inaction than verbal action on the part of *all* Christians when witnessing an anti-Jewish incident or hearing an anti-Jewish remark.

The majority of the Christians who report such anti-Jewish situations declare they dislike the hostility against the Jew expressed in these incidents or remarks, but they do not say anything to defend the Jew.

The majority of the Christians say they believe charges made against the Jew should be answered, but they themselves do not answer these charges.

None of the methods for changing the attitude of Christian toward Jew results in any more verbal action on the part of Christians in defending the Jew against anti-Jewish incidents or remarks.

Regardless of the methods used to influence attitudes, the least prejudiced Christians show only a slightly greater tendency than do other Christians to defend the Jew in various anti-Jewish situations.

CONCLUSION

As part of the present increased effort to reduce all group tensions in America, improving the relations between Christian and Jew is of great importance. While the majority of Christians in America are now neutral in their attitude toward the Jew, it is this very group which is most receptive to influences which may make it either more or less favorable in attitude toward the Jew. The success of anti-Semitism depends on the degree to which it can make this neutral group more anti-Jewish. Profoundly involved in the programs to make those presently neutral Christians *more favorable* in attitude toward the Jew are the theological theories that separate Christianity from Judaism as well as the religious figures and historical experiences which associate Christianity with Judaism. Methods in interfaith education designed to reduce prejudice between Christian and Jew must take into consideration the ambivalent nature of this religious affinity between Jew and Christian.

The popular techniques used by Christian and Jewish institutions in present-day interfaith education include (1) teaching the Jewish origins of Christianity; (2) reiterating the fact that the religious values of the Bible are held sacred by both Christian and Jew; (3) and preaching that the Bible's message of brotherly love professed by both Christian and Jew should motivate their relations. These popular techniques do not effectively decrease the degree of prejudice of Christian toward Jew. That this method does not *increase* anti-Jewish prejudice may refute psychoanalytic theory but it can hardly be of any practical satisfaction to educators who desire to decrease anti-Jewish attitudes.

A method which is effective in reducing the prejudice of Christian toward Jew is a Direct Group Method. The Direct Group Method (1) stimulates Christians in a group under authorized Christian religious influence to discuss directly pro and con their attitude toward the Jew; (2) it involves the Christian directly in the problem of Christian-Jewish relations; (3) it corrects misinformation about contemporary Jews; (4) it, in particular, gives opportunity in the group for the Christian's free expression of his personal experiences with Jews as a kind of group catharsis of hostility; and then, (5) it provides, under the guidance of the instructor, a reorientation of the Christian's values with reference to the Jew in the light of the common origins and moral beliefs of the "Judeo-Christian heritage." When the group evaluates its own expressed hostility, achieves insight into its stereotype thinking and makes its own decisions about the validity of its prejudgments, then the prejudice of the individual members in the group is significantly reduced.

Of the methods tested in this experiment, this Direct Group Method is the method which is not only the most effective in changing attitude of Christian toward Jew; it is also the method which results in the greater permanency of this changed attitude. This method does not adequately prepare the Christian, whose attitude toward the Jew has been made more favorable by its influence, to handle anti-Jewish incidents or defend Jews against anti-Jewish remarks. It does reduce this Christian's own receptivity to such anti-Jewish influences. It does increase this Christian's favorable participation in group discussions about Jews. In such discussions the Christian, whose attitude has been changed by this Direct Group Method, becomes himself active in improving the relations between Christian and Jew.

These findings have a bearing on the general problem of changing the attitudes of one group toward another. (1) They support those educators who contend that the best educational policy is to single out an intergroup tension for explicit attention. "To say as little as possible" about a specific conflict between groups only diminishes the effectiveness of the effort to improve attitudes. (2) The reconstruction of the attitudes of an in-group toward an out-group requires an active involvement of the individual of the in-group who must be made conscious that there is an intergroup problem. (3) The individuals of the in-group will offer less resistance to change in attitude if opportunity is provided for even a modest amount of free verbal expression of their repressed hostility to the out-group. (4) The cathartic effectiveness of this verbal release of aggression is greater when it is experienced in a group situation in which the individual has a sense of belonging. (5) To be utilized for changing attitudes the catharsis must be subject to a guided group discussion in which new attitudes in the individual may be effected by his group's approval of these new attitudes. (6) The emotional valences which the accepted moral and religious ideals of Christianity have for Christians in a consciously Christian group can under the favorable conditions described above be utilized to reorient a Christian's set of values with reference to an out-group. (7) The improvement in an individual's attitude toward an out-group will *not* fluctuate if it is reinforced by experiences which refer the changed attitude to the approval of one's own group. It *will* fluctuate if the change in attitude results from a single though favorable contact with a member of the out-group. (8) Finally, the findings in this experiment are related to the psychological investigations in attitudes conducted by the late Dr. Kurt Lewin and lend further support to his dynamic field theory of personality.

Our conclusions illustrate how the interpersonal forces within a group may be manipulated to change the attitudes of its individual members. We have demonstrated that interfaith educational programs should adopt *tested* group methods which *do* reduce prejudice. Educators and clergymen who are frequently called upon to participate in such programs should become acquainted with the new techniques in group dynamics which offer a more effective therapy for improving Christian-Jewish relations.

APPENDIX A

Form B

Please fill in the blanks: Do you live in a town _____ Large City _____

BOY _____   Month, Day, Year of your birth _____

GIRL _____   What work does your father do _____

THIS IS NOT A TEST! THERE ARE NO "RIGHT" OR "WRONG" ANSWERS. Put a circle around the answer which shows how *you feel* about each question. Since your name is not asked for be as straightforward as you can. If you agree with the question, circle "YES"; if you slightly agree with the question, circle "yes"; if you slightly disagree, circle "no"; if you disagree, circle "NO!"

1. Do you think that with a few exceptions most Jews are pretty much alike?
   YES!   yes   no   NO!

2. Do you think that Jews live in Jewish sections of cities because they are clannish and insist on sticking together?
   YES!   yes   no   NO!

3. Do you think that there are too many Jews in government positions?
   YES!   yes   no   NO!

4. Do you think that colleges and professional schools should limit the number of Jews they admit?
   YES!   yes   no   NO!

5. Do you think that Jews usually try to push ahead without considering the rights of others?
   YES!   yes   no   NO!

6. Do you think that Jews try, whenever possible, to get out of doing their share of any real hard work?
   YES!   yes   no   NO!

7. Do you think that we are indebted to the Jews for their contribution to religion?
   YES!   yes   no   NO!

8. Do you think that Jews control too much of the wealth of this country?
   YES!   yes   no   NO!

9. Do you think that people who are not Jewish should try to answer those
   who say things against the Jews?
   YES!   yes   no   NO!

10. Do you think that anyone who employs many people should be careful
    not to hire too many Jews?
    YES!   yes   no   NO!

11. Do you think that you would object if a member of your family wanted
    to marry a Jewish person?
    YES!   yes   no   NO!

12. Do you think that Jews should have as good a chance as others to get
    into any kind of work?
    YES!   yes   no   NO!

13. Do you think Jews did their fair share in the war?
    YES!   yes   no   NO!

14. Do you think that when Jews move into a nice section they spoil the
    neighborhood?
    YES!   yes   no   NO!

15. Do you think that Jews play a valuable part in American life?
    YES!   yes   no   NO!

16. Do you think you can tell whether a person you meet is Jewish?
    YES!   yes   no   NO!

17. How much experience have you had with Jews?
    none   very little   average   considerable

18. Do you have any Jewish friends?
    none   1 or 2   5   10

Form C
Information Sheet

Since your name is not asked for, please answer as frankly as you can. If you need more space use other side of this sheet.

WE UNDERSTAND THAT THIS PAST SUMMER YOU STUDIED THE PSALMS (or THE OLD TESTAMENT) WITH A RABBI AT YOUR YOUNG PEOPLE'S CONFERENCE.

1. What did you like best about the Rabbi's course:
   Check one: 1) The information he gave you _____
               2) The manner in which he taught _____
2. Did the Rabbi's course change any opinions you may have had about Jews?
          Yes _____ No _____
   If answer is yes—please state here what opinion (or opinions) was changed?
3. Since studying the Psalms (or Old Testament) with the Rabbi 8 months have passed. During this time, has there been any discussion or conversation about Jews in your church group?
          Yes _____ No _____
   If answer is yes, state here what it was about:
   What did you say?
4. During the past 8 months has there been any incident or remark concerning Jews which you witnessed or heard anywhere?
          Yes _____ No _____
   If answer is yes (omitting person's name) describe the incident or remark here:
   What did you think of the incident or remark?
   If you did or said anything in the situation, what did you do or say?

APPENDIX B

Some Correlates of Anti-Jewish Attitudes

ALLPORT AND KRAMER tested some of the "assertions regarding the etiology of prejudice" in their study of 437 college undergraduates (3). Their scale included eight items on attitudes toward the Jew selected from the Levinson-Sanford scale. Included in the information about their respondents with which their individual attitude scores were correlated were the degree of contact with Jews, sex differences, and religious training.

Allport and Kramer concluded that "religious training in itself does *not* lessen prejudice. But religious training which successfully stresses tolerance and brotherhood *does* tend to lessen prejudice" (Allport and Kramer, 1946, p. 38). Our study has proposed and tested two techniques in inter-religious education which do successfully lessen prejudice.

Regarding the sex variable in relation to anti-Jewish prejudice, we found as did Allport and Kramer that girls are less prejudiced than boys. The mean score on the attitudes scale for 342 girls was 15.72 as compared to a mean of 17.56 for 137 boys. The chi square of the difference in prejudice between the boys and the girls is 23.2 significant below the 1 percent level (see Table 1).

TABLE I

PERCENTAGE DISTRIBUTION OF BOYS AND GIRLS WHO FALL IN
THE FIRST QUARTILE, SECOND-THIRD QUARTILE, AND FOURTH
QUARTILE IN THE SCALE ON ATTITUDE TOWARD JEW

	N	Pro	Neutral	Anti
Girls	342	25.4	48.2	26.4
Boys	137	21.8	41.6	36.6

Harlan (1942) and Allport (Allport and Kramer, 1946) observed that casual experiences with the minority group did not diminish prejudice as markedly as did intimate equal status contact. This observation is corroborated by findings in this study. Table 2 indicates the mean attitude scores of groups in reference to four categories of friendship with Jews and four categories of experiences with Jews.

TABLE 2

MEAN ATTITUDE SCORES OF GROUPS IN THE CATEGORIES
OF NUMBER OF JEWISH FRIENDS

Total (N477)	None (N161)	1 or 2 (N161)	Five (N100)	Ten (N55)
16.02	18.72	15.34	14.15	13.42

MEAN ATTITUDE SCORES OF GROUPS IN THE CATEGORIES
OF EXPERIENCE WITH JEWS

Total (N477)	None (N63)	Very Little (N160)	Average (N193)	Considerable (N61)
16.02	18.72	16.83	14.94	15.67

Those who report no Jewish friends and no experience with Jews are the most prejudiced. Those who report an average amount of experience with Jews have a mean score slightly lower than those who report considerable experience. But, those who report five or ten Jewish friends are less anti-Jewish than those in all other categories.

When the most prejudiced are compared with the least prejudiced in attitude toward the Jew, this pattern of the influence of personal friendships with Jews as being greater than general contact with Jews in reducing prejudice is repeated (see Table 3).

TABLE 3

PERCENTAGE DISTRIBUTION OF THE NUMBER OF JEWISH
FRIENDS OF THOSE WHO FALL IN THE LEAST AND
THE MOST PREJUDICED CATEGORIES

	No Jewish Friends	1 or 2	Five	Ten
Most Prejudiced (N128)	41.6	32.8	15.3	10.3
Least Prejudiced (N125)	17.1	39.6	27.2	17.1

(The chi square is 22.3 significant at below the 1 percent level.)

PERCENTAGE DISTRIBUTION OF THE AMOUNT OF EXPERIENCE
WITH JEWS OF THOSE WHO FALL IN THE LEAST
AND THE MOST PREJUDICED CATEGORIES

	No Experience	*Little*	*Average*	*Considerable*
Most Prejudiced (N128)	17.2	32.8	35.8	14.2
Least Prejudiced (N125)	5.6	29.2	49.6	15.6

(The chi square is 7.8 significant at the 5 percent level.)

The highest percentage of the least prejudiced have one or two Jewish friends with an average amount of experience with Jews in general. The highest percentage of the most prejudiced have no Jewish friends with little to average amount of experience with Jews in general.

BIBLIOGRAPHY

Adorno, T. W. and Others. 1950. The Authoritarian Personality. (Studies in Prejudice; American Jewish Committee Social Studies Series. Publication No. 3). Harper, New York.

Allport, Gordon W. 1945. "Catharsis and the Reduction of Prejudice," *Journal of Social Issues,* I (3):3–10.

—— 1945. "Psychology of Participation," *Psychological Review,* 53: No. 3, pp. 117–132.

Allport, Gordon W., and Bernard M. Kramer. 1946. "Some Roots of Prejudice," *Journal of Psychology,* 22:9–39.

American Jewish Committee. 1949. Committee Reporter, 6, No. 1, New York, January.

Brameld, Theodore. 1946. Minority Problems in the Public Schools. Harper and Brothers. New York.

Campbell, D. W., and E. F. Stover. 1933. "Teaching International Mindedness in Social Studies." *Journal of Educational Sociology,* 7:244–248.

Chen, W. K. C. 1933. "The Influence of Oral Propaganda Material upon Students' Attitudes," *Archives of Psychology,* No. 150, New York.

Cherrington, Ben M. 1934. Methods of Education in International Attitudes. Contributions to Education, No. 595, Bureau of Publications, Teachers College, Columbia University.

Dollard, John et al. 1939. Frustration and Aggression. Yale University Press, New Haven.

Faris, E. 1935. "Sociology of Religious Strife," *Journal of Religion,* 15:207–219.

Frenkel-Brunswick, E., and R. N. Sanford. 1945. "Some Personality Factors in Anti-Semitism," *Journal of Psychology,* 20:271–291.

Freud, Sigmund. 1939. Moses and Monotheism. Alfred Knopf. New York.

Gardner, Iva C. 1935. "The Effect of a Group of Social Stimuli upon Attitudes," *Journal of Education Psychology,* 26:471–478.

Graeber, Isacque, and Stewart H. Britt, eds. 1942. Jews in a Gentile World. The Macmillan Co., New York.

Grayzel, Solomon. 1942. "Christian-Jewish Relations in the First Millennium," in *Essays on Anti-Semitism,* ed. by Koppel S. Pinson. Conference on Jewish Relations, New York.

Haggard, E. A., and R. J. Rose. 1944. "Some Effects of Mental Set and Active Participation in the Condition of the Auto-Kinetic Phenomenon," *Journal of Experimental Psychology,* 34:45–59.

Harlan, H. H. 1942. "Some Factors Affecting Attitude toward Jews," *American Sociological Review,* 7:816–827.

Hartman, G. W. 1936. "A Field Experiment on the Comparative Effectiveness of Emotional and Rational Political Leaflets in Determining Election Results," *Journal of Abnormal and Social Psychology,* 31:99–114.

Hay, M. V. 1950. Foot of Pride. Beacon Press, Boston.

Herford, R. Travers. 1924. The Pharisees. The Macmillan Co., New York.

Johnson, Charles S. 1946. "National Organizations in the Field of Race Relations," *The Annals,* 244:117–127.

Kagan, Henry E. 1944. "Anti-Semitism," *Religious Education,* 84–86, March.

Kalergi, H. Coudenhove. 1935. Anti-Semitism Throughout the Ages. Hutchinson, London.

Kay, Lillian Wald. 1947. "Frame of Reference in 'Pro' and 'Anti' Evaluation of Test Items," *Journal of Social Psychology,* 25:63–68.

Klausner, Joseph. 1929. Jesus of Nazareth, His Life, Times, and Teaching. The Macmillan Co., New York.

Knox, W. L. 1925. St. Paul and the Church of Jerusalem. Cambridge.

Kohler, Kaufmann. 1929. The Origins of the Synagogue and the Church. The Macmillan Co., New York.

Kuhlen, R. G., and M. Arnold. 1944. "Age Differences in Religious Beliefs and Problems during Adolescence." *Journal of Genetic Psychology,* 65:291–300.

Kulp, D. H. 1934. "Prestige as Measured by Single Experience Changes and Their Permanency," *Journal of Educational Research,* 27:663–672.

Levinson, D. J., and R. N. Sanford. 1944. "A Scale for the Measurement of Anti-Semitism," *Journal of Psychology,* 17:339–370.

Lewin, Kurt. 1943. "The Relative Effectiveness of a Lecture Method and a Method of Group Decision for Changing Food Habits," *National Research Council Bulletin,* No. 108, pp. 35–65.

—— 1944. "The Dynamics of Group Action," *Education Leadership,* I, 195–200.

Lewin, Kurt, and Paul Grabbe. 1945. "Conduct, Knowledge and Acceptance of New Values," *Journal of Social Issues,* I (3):53–64.

Likert, Rensis. 1932. A Technique for the Measurement of Attitudes. Archives of Psychology No. 140. Columbia University, New York.

Lippitt, Ronald, and Marian Radke. 1946. "New Trends in the Investigation of Prejudice," *The Annals,* 244:167–176.

Lorge, Irving. 1935. "Prestige, Suggestion, and Attitudes," *Psychological Bulletin,* Abstract, 32:750.

MacCrone, I. D. 1937. Race Attitudes in South Africa. Oxford University Press, London.

MacIver, R. M. 1948. The More Perfect Union. The Macmillan Co., New York.

McNemar, Quinn. 1946. "Opinion—Attitude Methodology." *Psychological Bulletin,* 43:289–374.

Maritain, Jacques. 1939. A Christian Looks at the Jewish Question. Longmans, Green, and Co., New York.

Marple, C. H. 1933. "The Comparative Susceptibility of Three Age Levels to the Suggestions of Group versus Expert Opinion," *Journal of Social Psychology,* 4:176–186.

Marrow, A. J., and John R. French Jr. 1945. "Changing a Stereotype in Industry," *Journal of Social Issues,* I (3).

Merton, Robert K., and Patricia L. Kendall. 1946. "The Focused Interview," *American Journal of Sociology,* 51:541–557.

Murphy, Gardner, and Rensis Likert. 1938. Public Opinion and the Individual. Harper, New York.

Oesterly, W. O. E. 1942. The Jews and Judaism during the Greek Period. London.

Parkes, James W. 1934. The Conflict of the Church and the Synagogue. Soncino Press, London.

—— 1938. The Jew in the Medieval Community. Soncino Press, London.

—— 1948. Judaism and Christianity. University of Chicago Press, Chicago.

Peterson, Ruth C., and L. L. Thurstone. 1933. Motion Pictures and the Social Attitudes of Children. The Macmillan Co., New York.

Rendall, C. H. 1927. The Epistle of St. James and Judaic Christianity. Cambridge.

Robinson, Duane, and Sylvia Rohde. 1945. "A Public Opinion Study of Anti-Semitism in New York City," *American Sociological Review,* 10:511–515.

—— 1946. "Two Experiments with an Anti-Semitism Poll," *Journal of Abnormal and Social Psychology,* 41:136–144.

Rose, Arnold M. 1947. Studies in Reduction of Prejudice. Chicago: American Council on Race Relations. Mimeographed.

Saadi, M., and P. R. Fransworth. 1934. "The Degree of Acceptance of Dogmatic Statements and Preferences for Their Supposed Makers," *Journal of Abnormal and Social Psychology,* 29:143–150.

Samuel, Maurice. 1940. The Great Hatred. Knopf, New York.

Sherif, Muzafer. 1936. The Psychology of Social Norms. Harper and Brothers, New York.

Sherif, Muzafer, and Hadley Cantril. 1945–1946. "The Psychology of 'Attitudes,'" Part I, *Psychological Review*, 52:295–319, 1945; Part II, *Psychological Review*, 53:1–25, 1946.

—— 1947. The Psychology of Ego-Involvements. John Wiley & Sons, New York.

Simmel, Ernst, ed. 1946. Anti-Semitism, A Social Disease. International University Press, New York.

Sletto, R. F. 1937. Construction of Personality Scales by the Criterion of Internal Consistency. The Sociological Press, Minneapolis.

Smith, F. Tredwell. 1943. An Experiment in Modifying Attitudes towards the Negro. Teachers College, Columbia University, New York.

Sorokin, P. A., and J. W. Boldgreff. 1932. "An Experimental Study of the Influence of Suggestion on the Discrimination and the Valuation of People," *American Journal of Sociology*, 37:720–737.

Trachtenberg, Joshua. 1943. The Devil and the Jews: The Medieval Conception of the Jew and Its Relation to Modern Anti-Semitism. Yale.

Valentin, Hugo. 1936. Anti-Semitism Historically and Critically Examined. Viking Press, New York.

Van Tuyl, M. C. T. 1938. "Where Do the Students 'Lose' Religion," *Religious Education*, 33:19–29.

Watson, Goodwin. 1946. Action for Unity. Harper and Brothers, New York.

Williams, Robin M., Jr. 1947. The Reduction of Intergroup Tensions: A Survey of Research on Problems of Ethnic, Racial and Religious Group Relations. Social Science Research Council, Bulletin 57, New York.

Young, Donald. 1927. "Some Effects of a Course in American Race Problems on the Race Prejudice of 450 Undergraduates at the University of Pennsylvania," *Journal of Abnormal and Social Psychology*, 22:235–242.

INDEX

Abraham, the first Jew, 67, 85; treatment of strangers, 89

Aggression, interlocking factors causing: targets for, and displacement of, 3; verbal catharsis, 20, 54, 138

Allport, Gordon W., Foreword, vii ff., quoted, 15, 20

—— and B. M. Kramer, minority attitudes study, 19, 27, 28, 142

America, equality involved in political democracy of, 1; minorities in, 2, 42; effort to reduce group tensions: Christians' neutrality toward Jews, 136

Amos, prophet, 70

Antagonisms, intergroup: efforts and organizations striving to modify, 2, 136; see also Attitudes

Anti-Jewish attitude, age at which begins, 19; courses designed to reduce, within Christian group, 24, 36 f., 58 ff.; defined: how differs from anti-Semitism, 28; see also Attitudes

Anti-Semitism, functions in, but incompatible with, Western Christian society, 1 ff.; interlocking factors in complex phenomenon of, 4; religious aspect, 4 ff.; differentiation of medieval and modern, 9; Nazi, 9 f., 13, 46, 87; now called the "Christian problem," 11; psychoanalytic approach to, 12 ff.; Freudian theory, 12; Levinson-Sanford Scale for measuring, 14 f., 27, 132; difference between anti-Jewish attitude and, 28; efforts to reduce, in America, 136

Attitudes, efforts to reduce group tensions, 2, 136; recent investigations, 17, 26, 27, 32, 138; processes leading to modification and reconstruction of, 20; relation of verbal behavior (q.v.) to change in, 102-28

—— of Christians toward Jews, problem of how to change: religious frame of reference, 1-15, 136; three methods for influencing and determining, 15-23; courses designed to reduce, 24, 36 f., 58 ff.; scale for measuring, 26-35, 131 f. (apx., 139-44); method that did not change attitudes, 42 ff., 57, 72, 93 f. (see Indirect Group Method); methods that did change them, 53, 57, 84, 90, 93 f. (see Direct Group Method; Focused Private Interview); stability of change, 95-101; relation of verbal behavior to change, 102-28; summary, 129-35; conclusion, 136-38; see also Anti-Jewish attitude; Anti-Semitism; also entries mentioned above, e.g., Methods; Scales; Verbal; etc.

Augustine, Saint, quoted, 59

Babylonian Exile, 66

Balaam's Curse, 69

Barnabas, epistle of, 59

Beard, Miriam, quoted, 3

Berlin, Irving, 47

Bible, emotional valence: its prestige and influence, 16; the stimulus material used by Rabbis in teaching Christians, 18; beliefs of modern Christian and Jew inherited from writers of, 38, 129; "Old Testament" the background for Christians' acceptance of, 58; Jewish origin: historical evolution of the thirty-nine books, 64; three Jewish divisions: why Judaism and, preserved, 67; see also Old Testament; Psalms; Torah